# AMERICAN

# SYMBOLS

## COMMEMORATIVE EDITION

### DEBBIE SENNETT

Written and designed by Debbie Sennett.

This book is specially dedicated to my mother,
father and husband whose
encouragement and support made it possible.

Debbie Sennett

National Library of Canada Cataloguing in Publication

Sennett, Deborah, 1952-
 American symbols : commemorative edition / Deborah Sennett.
ISBN 1-55369-319-1
 1. Heraldry--United States--States.  I. Title.
CR203.A42 2002          929.6'0973          C2002-901250-3

# TRAFFORD

**This book was published *on-demand* in cooperation with Trafford Publishing.**
On-demand publishing is a unique process and service of making a book available for retail sale to the public taking advantage of on-demand manufacturing and Internet marketing.
**On-demand publishing** includes promotions, retail sales, manufacturing, order fulfilment, accounting and collecting royalties on behalf of the author.

Suite 6E, 2333 Government St., Victoria, B.C. V8T 4P4, CANADA
Phone      250-383-6864       Toll-free    1-888-232-4444 (Canada & US)
Fax        250-383-6804       E-mail      sales@trafford.com
Web site    www.trafford.com   TRAFFORD PUBLISHING IS A DIVISION OF TRAFFORD'
HOLDINGS LTD.
Trafford Catalogue #02-0132     www.trafford.com/robots/02-0132.html

10     9     8     7     6     5     4     3     2

# CONTENTS

# AMERICAN
# SYMBOLS

## COMMEMORATIVE EDITION

Is dedicated to the memory
of all the people whose
self sacrifice, courage and daring
made the United States of America
the great country it is today.

# American Symbols Commemorative Edition

## Introduction

American Symbols Commemorative Edition has the common information about the different state flowers, birds and trees as well as information about the many new symbols which the states have enacted including their dates of inception and scientific names. It is however important to note that since our laws are constantly being created, revised and debated, there may seem to be discrepancies in some of the symbols inception dates. Also, it is important to note that since their inception, some of the symbols have had their scientific names changed by the scientific community. Please do keep in mind that it is not uncommon for a symbol to have several inception dates and more than one correct scientific name. Should you require additional information to avoid confusion it may be necessary to check with the individual state for any current legislation and with the scientific community for any recent name changes.

To commemorate the year 2000 American Symbols Commemorative Edition also includes the active and colorful history of each of the states and interesting facts and trivia about each of the states. As author of this keepsake edition I have taken great care in compiling the information in this book to insure its value to you in your personal library. I sincerely hope you enjoy reading American Symbols Commemorative Edition as much as I enjoyed writing it.

Debbie Sennett

# ALABAMA

Alabama:  In the Creek Indian language Alabama means tribal town.
Capital:  Montgomery
Flower:  Red camellia or any camellia (*Camellia*) 1959
Wildflower:  Oak leaf hydrangea (*Hydrangea quercifolia*) 1999
Tree:  Southern longleaf pine (*Pinus palustris*) 1997
Bird:  Yellowhammer (*Colaptes auratus*) 1927
Game Bird:  Wild turkey (*Meleagris gallopavo*) 1980
Nickname:  The Heart of Dixie, The Camellia State or The Cotton State
Rank:  22 (December 14, 1819)
Motto:  *Audermus jura nostra defendere* (We dare defend our rights)
        1939
Creed:  Alabama Creed 1953
Song:  Alabama by Julia S. Tutwiler and Edna Gockel Gussen 1933
Folk Dance:  Square dance 1981
Gemstone:  Star blue quartz 1990
Mineral:  Red iron ore (*Hematite*) 1967
Rock:  Marble 1969
Shell:  Johnstone's junonia (*Scaphella junonia johnstoneae*) 1990
Fossil:  Archaeocete whale (*Basilosaurus cetoides*), Eocene 1984
Soil:  Bama soil series 1997
Horse:  Racking horse (*Equus caballus*) 1975
Insect:  Monarch butterfly (*Danaus plexippus*) 1989
Mascot:  Eastern tiger swallowtail butterfly (*Pterourus glaucus*) 1989
Reptile:  Red bellied turtle (*Pseudemys alabamensis*) 1990
Amphibian:  Red hills salamander (*Phaeognathus hubrichti*), endangered
        2000
Freshwater Fish:  Largemouth  bass (*Micropterus salmoides*) 1975
Saltwater Fish:  Tarpon (*Megalops atlanticus*) 1955
Nut:  Pecan (*Carya illinoensis*) 1982
Bible:  Alabama State Bible 1853
Quilt:  Pine burr quilt 1997
Championship:  Alabama Championship Horse Show 1988
Horseshoe Tournament:  Stockton Fall Horseshoe Tournament 1992
Agricultural Museum:  Dothan Landmark Park 1992
Barbeque Championship:  Demopolis Christmas on the River 1991
Historic Theater:  Alabama Theater for the Performing Arts 1993
Outdoor Drama:  *The Miracle Worker* by William Gibson 1991
Outdoor Musical Drama:  *The Incident at Looney's Tavern* 1993
Renaissance Faire:  Florence Renaissance Faire 1988
Colors:  Red and white
Poets Laureate:  Alabama State Poets Laureate 1930
Coat of Arms:  Alabama Coat of Arms

# HISTORY

In 6000 B. C. Russell Cave was inhabited by humans.

Hernando de Soto fought with the Tuscaloosa Indians in 1540.

The French made the first permanent settlement of Alabama on Mobile Bay in 1702.

Britain ceded the region to the United States after the War for Independence with the Treaty of Paris in 1783.

The United States was ceded land by the Chickasaws, Choctaws and Cherokees in 1805.

Creek Indians were defeated by General Andrew Jackson in 1814 at the battle of Horseshoe Bend. The Creeks were relocated to Oklahoma.

The state of Alabama was organized as a territory in 1817.

In 1853 the executive department purchased the State Bible. The State Bible is used for the inauguration of Alabama governors.

On January 11, 1861 Alabama seceded from the Union.

Jefferson Davis was inaugurated as President of the provisional government of the Confederate States of America in 1861.

Admiral David Farragut issued the famous command "Damn the torpedoes, full speed ahead," at the battle of Mobile Bay on August 5, 1864.

In 1868 Alabama was readmitted to the Union.

Tuskegee Institute was founded in 1881 by Booker T. Washington.

In 1955 there was a bus boycott in Montgomery.

Black freedom advocates marched from Selma to Montgomery in 1965.

# FACTS AND TRIVIA

The rural economy of growing cotton had to be diversified in 1915 because of the boll weevil. This destructive insect caused farmers to grow crops other than cotton. There is a boll weevil monument in Enterprise.

Russell Cave National Monument near Bridgeport preserves a shelter built by prehistoric Indians. A prehistoric skeleton was found in the cave.

Jefferson Davis memorabilia is exhibited in Montgomery.

Mobile is host to the annual America's Junior Miss contest. The contest began in 1958.

The Rocket Capital of the World is in Huntsville. The first rocket that put man on the moon was built in Alabama.

A 60 ton statue of Vulcan, the Roman god of fire, overlooks Birmingham.

The Confederate States of America was born in Montgomery. In 1861 the Confederate flag was designed and first flown in Alabama.

In Fort Payne the musical singing group Alabama has a Museum.

Bellingrath Gardens near Mobile has year round displays of flowers.

The Hall of History in Bessemer exhibits the typewriter Hitler used at his mountain retreat.

Mardi Gras was first introduced in Mobile, Alabama. The day before Lent, which is called Shrove or Fat Tuesday is Mardi Gras Day.

# ALASKA

Alaska:  The name Alaska is derived from the Aleut word *alyesk* which means great land.

Capital:  Juneau

Flower:  Forget-me-not (*Myosotis alpestris*) 1917

Tree:  Sitka spruce (*Picea sitchensis*) 1962

Bird:  Willow ptarmigan (*Lagopus lagopus*) 1955

Nickname:  The Last Frontier or The Land of the Midnight Sun

Rank:  49 (January 3, 1959)

Motto:  North to the Future 1967

Song:  Alaska's Flag by Marie Drake and Elinor Dusenbury 1955

Gem:  Jade 1968

Mineral:  Gold (*Au*) 1968

Fossil:  Woolly mammoth (*Mammuthus primigenius*), Pleistocene 1986

Land Mammal:  Moose (*Alces alces*) 1998

Insect:  Four spot skimmer dragonfly (*Libellula quadrimaculata*) 1995

Marine Mammal:  Bowhead whale (*Balaena mysticetus*), endangered 1983

Fish:  Giant king salmon or chinook salmon (*Oncorhynchus tshawytscha*) 1962

Sport:  Mushing or dog team racing 1972

# HISTORY

The Bering Sea land bridge was used for the earliest migration from Asia to America over 15,000 years ago. The Eskimos, Aleuts, Tlingits and Tinnehs inhabited Alaska.

In 1728 Peter the Great sent an expedition to find land opposite Siberia. Vitus Bering discovered Alaska in 1741.

Three Saints Bay was the site of the first Russian settlement in 1784.

Sitka was made the capital of Russian America in 1799.

In 1802 the Tlingits were massacred at Sitka. The massacre was called Baranov's massacre.

Gold was discovered in Alaska at Stikine Creek (1861), Juneau (1880), Fortymile Creek (1886), Nome (1898) and Fairbanks (1903).

The United States purchased Alaska from Russia in 1867 for two cents per acre or 7.2 million dollars. Czar Alexander II sold Alaska to the U. S. to prevent its capture by the British. The acquisition was called Seward's Folly after the United States Secretary of State William H. Seward.

In 1878 the first salmon cannery was established.

Agattu, Attu and Kiska Islands were occupied by the Japanese in 1942. The United States expelled the Japanese in 1943 with their Alaskan defenses.

Cook Inlet, the Northwest Panhandle and Anchorage were destroyed by an earthquake in 1964.

Valdez was destroyed by tsunami in 1964.

The Kodiak coast sank 32 feet and Seward rose 16 feet in 1964.

Oil was discovered in 1968.

In 1971 Alaska's Native Americans were given 44 million acres for their native landholdings.

The 789 mile oil pipeline to Valdez was completed in 1977.

In 1989 the worst oil spill in U. S. history occurred when the Exxon Valdez spilled 10 million gallons of oil into the Prince William Sound off the coast of Valdez.

## FACTS AND TRIVIA

The Alaska gold rush began with Joe Juneau's 1880 discovery.

Oil and natural gas are Alaska's most important sources of revenue. Alaska produces 25% of the oil in the United States.

The largest private industry in Alaska is the fishing and seafood industry. Alaska supplies most of the salmon, crab, herring and halibut for the U. S.

Mt. McKinley is the highest point in North America at 20,320 feet above sea level. Alaska has 17 of the 20 highest peaks in the United States.

The largest national forest in the United States is the Tongass National Forest in Alaska.

In 1915 at Fort Yukon the record high temperature was 100 degrees Fahrenheit. Prospect Creek Camp had the record low temperature of -80 degrees Fahrenheit in 1971.

Mount Cleveland erupted near Anchorage in 1994.

# ARIZONA

Arizona: The name Arizona is thought to have been derived from the Pima or Papago Indian language and means place of small springs.

Capital: Phoenix

Flower: Seguaro cactus blossom (*Carnegiea gigantia*) 1901, 1931 and 1973

Tree: Palo verde (*Cercidium*) 1973

Bird: Cactus wren (*Campylorhynchyus brunneicapillus*) 1931 and 1973

Nickname: The Grand Canyon State

Rank: 48 (February 14, 1912)

Motto: *Ditat Deus* (God enriches)

Song: The Arizona March Song (Arizona) by Margaret Rowe Clifford and Maurice Blumenthal 1919

Gemstone: Turquoise 1974

Fossil: Petrified wood (*Araucarioxylon arizonicum*), Triassic 1988

Mammal: Ringtail (*Bassariscus astutus*) 1986

Fish: Apache trout (*Oncorhynchus apache*) 1986

Reptile: Arizona ridge nosed rattlesnake (*Crotalus willardi*) 1986

Amphibian: Arizona tree frog (*Hyla eximia*) 1986

Colors: Blue and old gold 1915

Neckwear: Bola tie 1973

# HISTORY

Highly advanced cultures of Indians developed in Arizona during prehistoric times. Cliff cities built by these cultures were abandoned during the thirteenth century during a great 30 year drought. The Pueblo Indians were replaced by the Apaches and Navajos.

The first Spanish explorers were Alvar Nunez Cabeza de Vaca in 1536 and Marcos de Niza in 1539.

Arizona was under Spanish rule from 1598-1821 as part of New Spain.

In 1638 missionaries lived among the Hopi Indians.

The first European settlement was Tubac in 1752.

In 1821 all of the Mexican settlements were destroyed by Apaches except for Tucson. Arizona was ceded by Spain to Mexico in 1821.

After the Mexican War in 1848, the northern part of Arizona was ceded to the United States by the Treaty of Guadalupe Hidalgo.

The Gadsden Purchase in 1853 granted the area south of Gila River to the United States.

Arizona was organized as a territory in 1863.

In 1886 Geronimo's surrender put an end to the Apache wars.

Roosevelt Dam was built in 1911 on Salt River.

The right to vote was granted to Native Americans in 1948.

Glen Canyon Dam was built in 1964 on the Colorado River.

## FACTS AND TRIVIA

The Arizona State Capital Museum has a symbols exhibit. The exhibit features objects which can be touched and information written in Braille.

There are eleven species of rattlesnakes found in Arizona.

Grand Canyon National Park is located in Arizona. The park's Flaming Gorge has twelve hundred foot high walls of red and orange. Marble Canyon has a one thousand foot thick seam of marble and the canyon's Disaster Falls is actually the site of an early explorers wreck.

Kitts Peak National Observatory is located in Sells. The observatory houses the largest solar telescope in the world.

The largest American cactus is the saguaro cactus. Syrup is made from the saguaro fruit which is harvested by the Pima and Papago Indians.

It would take about 4,800,000 pennies to equal the amount of copper on the roof of the Arizona capital building. Bisbee in Tombstone Canyon is called the "Queen of the Copper Mines".

Window Rock is the capital of the Navajo reservation.

Hopi Indians in Arizona founded Oraibi which is the oldest Indian settlement in the United States.

The original London Bridge was shipped to Lake Havasu City and reconstructed stone by stone.

The Petrified Forest is located in northeastern Arizona. Most petrified wood comes from the Petrified Forest.

# ARKANSAS

Arkansas: The name Arkansas originated from the Sioux Indian word *acansa* which means downstream place or from the Quapaw Indian word *akansea* which means south wind.

Capital: Little Rock

Flower: Apple blossom (*Malus*) 1901

Tree: Pine (Pinus) 1939

Bird: Mockingbird (*Mimus polyglottos*) 1929

Nickname: The Land of Opportunity, The Razorback State or The Natural State

Rank: 25 (June 15, 1836)

Motto: *Regnat Populus* (The people rule) 1836

Creed: Arkansas Creed 1972

Historical Song: The Arkansas Traveler by Sanford Faulkner 1987

Songs: Arkansas (You Run Deep In Me) by Wayland Holyfield 1987
Oh, Arkansas by Terry Rose and Gary Klaff 1987

Anthem: Arkansas by Mrs. Eva Ware Barnett 1987

Folk Dance: Square dance 1991

Instrument: Fiddle 1985

Gem: Diamond 1967

Rock: Bauxite 1967

Mineral: Quartz crystal 1967

Mammal: White tailed deer (*Odocoileus virginianus*) 1993

Insect: Honeybee (*Apis mellifera*) 1973

Fish: Rainbow darter (*Etheostoma caeruleum*), Unofficial*

Beverage: Milk 1985

Fruit and Vegetable: South Arkansas vine ripe pink tomato 1987

# HISTORY

In 500 A. D. bluff dwellers were present. They were replaced by mound building cultures.

Hernando de Soto explored the region for Spain in 1541.

Louis Jolliet and Jacques Marquette explored the region in 1673.

The region was claimed by Rene Robert de La Salle for France in 1682.

Arkansas Post the first permanent settlement was founded by Henri de Tonti on the Arkansas River in 1686.

France yielded the land to Spain in 1782. It was given back to France by Spain in 1800 and France ceded the region to the United States in 1803 as part of the Louisiana Purchase.

The region was organized into a territory from part of the Missouri Territory in 1819.

Arkansas joined the Confederate States of America on May 6, 1861.

Little Rock was captured by the Union Army in 1863.

In 1887 Bauxite was discovered.

Federal troops were sent to Little Rock in 1957 to insure desegregation.

The Mississippi River system was linked to Arkansas and Oklahoma by the McClellan Kerr Arkansas River Navigation System in 1971.

# FACTS AND TRIVIA

Many of the early apple trees in northern Arkansas were planted by John Chapman. John Chapman was also known as Johnny Appleseed. There is an annual Arkansas Apple Festival in Lincoln.

The annual Christmas lights display in Little River at the County Courthouse has made the town famous.

Arkansas has six national park sites, seven national scenic byways, fifty state parks and three state scenic byways.

Over one million acres comprise the Ozark National Forest. There are two and a half million acres of national forests in Arkansas. The oldest national forest in the south is the Ouachita National Forest.

Wal-Mart stores was founded by Sam Walton in Bentonville.

Crater of Diamonds State Park is in Murfreesboro. Diamonds, garnets, jasper, quartz, amethyst and agate can be prospected for at the park.

It is reported that the Magnet Cove region in Arkansas contains 102 different types of minerals.

The Arkansas River is 1,450 miles long.

Eureka Springs is home to the largest freestanding rock formation. The base of the formation is only 10 inches but the top measures approximately 10 feet across.

Stuttgart is host to the annual World Championship Duck Calling Contest.

Hot Springs Mountain has 47 hot springs that flow from its southwestern slope. The water from these hot springs has an average temperature of 143 degrees. Hot Springs, Arkansas is the boyhood home of President Bill Clinton.

# CALIFORNIA

California: The name California is thought to have been derived from a mythical island in the 16th century romance, *The Deeds of Esplandidn*. The book was published in 1510 by Garcia Ordonez de Montalvo.

Capital: Sacramento

Flower: Golden California poppy (*Eschsholtzia californicus*) 1903

Tree: Coast redwood (*Sequois sempervirens*) 1937
    Sierra big tree (*Sequoia gigantea*) 1953

Bird: California valley quail (*Lophortyx californica*) 1931

Nickname: The Golden State (1968), The Land of Milk and Honey, The El Dorado State and The Grape State

Rank: 31 (September 9, 1850)

Motto: *Eureka* (I have found it)   Gold was discovered in the Sierra Nevada. 1963

Song: I Love You, California by F. B. Silverwood and A. F. Frankenstein 1988

Dance: West coast swing dance 1988

Folk Dance: Square dance 1988

Fife and Drum Band: California Consolidated Drum Band 1997

Gemstone: Blue diamond (*Benitoite*) 1985

Rock: Serpentine 1965

Mineral: Gold (*Au*) 1965

Fossil: Sabre-toothed cat (*Smilodon fatalis or californicus*), Pleistocene 1973

Prehistoric Artifact: Chipped stone bear 1991

Soil: San joaquin soil 1997

Animal: California grizzly bear (*Ursus californicus*), extinct 1953

Insect: California dog face butterfly (*Zerene eurydice*) 1972

Marine Mammal: California gray whale (*Eschrichtius robustus*) 1975

Reptile: Desert tortoise (*Gopherus agasizzi*) 1972

Fish: California golden trout (*Oncorhynchus aguabonita*) 1947

Marine Fish: Garibaldi (*Hypsypops rubicundus*) 1995

Colors: Blue and gold 1951

Theater: Pasadena Playhouse 1937

Poet Laureate: Charles B. Garrigus 1966

Poppy Day: The 6th of April 1996

Poppy Week: May 13-18 1996

# HISTORY

Juan Rodrigues Cabrillo landed at San Diego Bay in 1542.

San Francisco Bay was the site where Francis Drake landed in 1579.

Missions were founded at San Diego in 1769, Monterey in 1770, San Luis Obispo in 1772 and San Juan Capistrano in 1778.

In 1823 California became part of independent Mexico.

John C. Fremont set up the Bear Flag Republic and captured Sonoma in 1846 starting the war between the United States and Mexico. Mexico ceded California to the United States in the Treaty of Guadalupe Hidalgo in 1848.

In 1848 a lumberjack named James Marshall found gold nuggets on the American River while building a sawmill for John Sutter. The famous "Forty-niner" gold rush which peaked in 1852 brought over 80,000 miners into the state causing rapid development in California.

There were 452 people killed and 28,000 buildings destroyed in 1906 as a result of the San Francisco earthquake.

Japanese were prohibited from holding land in 1913 by the Webb Alien Land Law.

California has been the largest state by population since 1963.

Property tax was limited by Proposition 13 in 1978.

There were 67 people killed and 48,000 left homeless on October 17, 1989 as a result of the Loma Prieta earthquake. The earthquake was the second most powerful in U. S. history measuring 7.1 on the Richter scale. The Loma Prieta earthquake caused over 10 billion dollars in property damage.

# FACTS AND TRIVIA

The state of California is a leader in agriculture despite the alarming lack of water. The Imperial Valley is irrigated by drawing off 4.4 million acre feet from the Colorado River and almost the entire flow of the San Joaquin River.

California has suffered 8 major earthquakes during the 20th century. There are over 500,000 seismic tremors detected in California each year.

The largest outdoor amphitheater in the world is the Hollywood Bowl.

Kings Canyon National Park in California is home to the nation's national Christmas tree. The giant sequoia tree was given this honor in 1925 and is over 300 feet in height.

More than 300,000 tons of grapes are grown in California each year. There are over 17 million gallons of wine produced each year in California.

The hottest and driest place in the United States is Death Valley.

An annual Avocado Festival is held in Fallbrook, California. Fallbrook is called the Avocado Capital of the World, the Coachella Valley is called the Date Capital of the World and Fresno is called the Raisin Capital of the World.

Kennedy Mine in Jackson, California was the deepest mine in North America and one of the richest gold mines in the world in the late 1850's.

On April 2, 1902 the first motion picture theater opened in Los Angeles.

Joanne Woodward was the first to receive a star on the Hollywood Walk of Fame in 1960.

# COLORADO

Colorado:  The word Colorado is Spanish for colored red.
Capital:  Denver
Flower:  Rocky Mountain columbine (*Aquilegia caerules*) 1899
Tree:  Colorado blue spruce (*Picea pungens*) 1939
Bird:  Lark bunting (*Calamospiza melanocorys stejneger*) 1931
Nickname:  The Centennial State or Colorful Colorado
Rank:  38 (August 1, 1876)
Motto:  *Nil Sine Numine* (Nothing without the deity)
Song:  Where The Columbines Grow by A. J. Flynn 1915
Folk Dance:  Square dance 1992
Gemstone:  Aquamarine 1971
Fossil:  Stegosaurus dinosaur (*Stegosaurus stenops*), Jurassic 1982
Animal:  Rocky Mountain bighorn sheep (*Ovis canadensis*) 1961
Insect:  Colorado hairstreak butterfly (*Hypaurotis cysalus*) 1996
Fish:  Greenback cutthroat trout (*Oncorhynchus clarki somias*) 1994
Grass:  Blue grama grass 1987

# HISTORY

Cliff dwellings were built by Pueblo Indians through the 1200's.

The region was settled by the Arapaho and the Cheyenne Indians after the 13th century.

In 1763 France abandoned its claim of the region. France's claim was reinstated in 1801 by Spain. The United States acquired Colorado as part of the Louisiana Purchase in 1803 and as part of the Mexican cession in 1848.

The area was explored by Zebulon Pike for the United States in 1806.

John Fremont and Major Stephen Long explored the region from 1820-1850.

San Luis was the first permanent settlement in 1851.

Gold was discovered in 1858 at Cherry Creek west of Denver.

Colorado was organized as a territory in 1861.

There were 400 Cheyenne killed at the Sand Creek Massacre in 1864. The Cheyenne and Utes Indians fought white settlement through the 1870's.

Silver and lead was discovered in 1875.

In 1906 the United States mint opened in Denver.

Near Grand Junction uranium was discovered in 1946.

# FACTS AND TRIVIA

Arapaho Indians and Cheyenne or Plains Indians were the native peoples of eastern Colorado. While the Utes or Great Basin Indians were the native peoples of western Colorado.

In Deer Trail the world's first rodeo was held on July 4, 1869.

Colorado is the only state in history to decide not to host the Olympics.

The economy of Colorado is a mixture of technology and agriculture in the east along with ski tourism and mining in the mountains.

Colorado has a limited water supply which hinders the states economic development in resource extraction.

The high altitude of Colorado doubles the effect of auto emissions.

It took six years to install the Beulah red marble in the Colorado State Capitol. The marble cannot be replaced because all of the Beulah red marble in the world was used in the construction of the Capitol.

The longest street in America is Colfax Avenue in Denver, Colorado.

Great Sand Dunes National Monument in Alamosa, Colorado is the tallest sand dune in America.

"America the Beautiful" was written by Katherine Lee Bates inspired by the view from Pikes Peak.

Royal Gorge is home to the highest suspension bridge in the world.

The longest tunnel in the United States is the E. Johnson Memorial tunnel. The tunnel is 8,959 feet long.

Leadville, Colorado is the highest incorporated city in the United States.

In 1820 Erwin James lead the 1st party to climb Pikes Peak. Colorado has 75% of the land with an altitude over 10,000 feet.

Grand Mesa is home to the largest flat top mountain in the world.

# CONNECTICUT

Connecticut:  Connecticut is a Mahican word meaning beside the long tidal river.

Capital:  Hartford

Flower:  Mountain laurel (*Kalmia latifolia*) 1907

Tree:  Charter oak or white oak (*Quercus alba*) 1947

Bird:  American robin (*Turdus migratorius*) 1943

Nickname:  The Constitution State or The Nutmeg State

Rank:  5 (January 9, 1788)

Motto:  *Qui Transtulit Sustinet* (He who transplanted still sustains)

Song:  Yankee Doodle 1978

Folk Dance:  Square dance 1995

Mineral:  Garnet or almandine garnet 1977

Fossil:  Three toed dinosaur track (*Eubrontes giganteus*), Triassic 1991

Animal:  Sperm whale (*Physeter macrosephalus*) 1975

Insect:  European praying mantis (*Mantis religiosa*) 1977

Shellfish:  Eastern oyster (*Crassostrea virginica*) 1989

Fish:  Brook trout (*Salvelinus fontinalis*), Unofficial*

Ship:  *USS Nautilus* (SSN-571) 1983

Heroine:  Prudence Crandall 1995

Hero:  Nathan Hale 1985

Composer: Charles Ives 1991

Poet Laureate:  Leo Connellan 1996-2001 (appointed for 5 years)

Troubadour:  Hugh Blumenfeld 2000 (appointed bi-annually)

# HISTORY

Adriaen Block claimed the region for the Dutch in 1614.

In Hartford a Dutch trading post was established in 1633.

Colonies were started by Plymouth Bay settlers in 1634 along the Connecticut River.

Pequot Indians were defeated in 1637.

The royal charter of 1662 was hidden in 1667 by Captain Joseph Wadsworth to prevent armed forces dispatched by King James II from seizing the document. The white oak that hid the charter fell during a storm in 1856. This majestic white oak tree had come to be known as the Charter Oak.

During the Revolutionary War the British governor supported the colonists and remained in office. The Continental Army received a large amount of supplies from Connecticut.

The six shooter was invented by Samuel Colt in 1835.

In 1844 the first anesthesia was used by Horace Wells.

The sewing machine was invented by Elias Howe in 1845.

Ella T. Grasso became the first woman governor in 1974.

# FACTS AND TRIVIA

Both Benedict Arnold the traitor and Nathan Hale the patriot were natives of Connecticut.

The first dictionary was published in Connecticut.

In 1776, "My only regret is that I have but one life to give for my country," were the famous last words of school teacher Nathan Hale before he was hung by the British as a spy.

Groton is where the 1st atomic powered submarine was built.

Connecticut was first to issue permanent license plates for cars in 1937.

In 1901 Connecticut passed the first automobile speed limit law. The law set the speed limit at 12 miles per hour.

The state of Connecticut has the highest per capita income.

Stamford, Connecticut is headquarters for the World Wrestling Federation (WWF).

John Brown the abolitionist was a native of Connecticut.

The state shellfish or the eastern oyster is cultivated in the waters of the Long Island Sound. In 1890 the largest fleet of oyster steamers in the world were in Connecticut.

Harriet Beecher Stowe the author was a native of Connecticut.

Connecticut's state insect, the praying mantis, is a beneficial insect that feeds on harmful insects such as moths, grasshoppers, aphids and caterpillars.

Eli Whitney the inventor was a native of Connecticut.

Calico bush and spoonwood are other names for the mountain laurel. The state flower of Connecticut is the mountain laurel.

It is illegal to walk across the street on your hands in Hartford.

The Hartford Courant is the oldest newspaper in the United States. It was established in 1764.

# DELAWARE

Delaware:  The state of Delaware is named for the Delaware River which was named for Sir Thomas West, Lord De La Warre, colonial governor of Virginia.

Capital:  Dover

Flower:  Peach blossom (*Prunus persica*) 1895

Tree:  American holly (*Ilex opaca aiton*) 1939

Bird:  Blue hen chicken (*Gallus*) 1939

Nickname:  The First State, The Diamond State, The Blue Hen State or Small Wonder

Rank:  1 (December 7, 1787)

Motto:  Liberty and Independence

Song:  Our Delaware by George B. Hynson, Donn Devine and Will M. S. Brown 1925

Mineral:  Sillimanite 1977

Fossil:  Belemnite or extinct squid with a conical shell (*Belemnitella americana*), Cretaceous 1996

Bug:  Ladybug or convergent ladybird beetle (*Hippodamia convergens*) 1974

Fish:  Weakfish, sea trout, yellow fin trout or tide runner (*Cynoscion regalis*) 1981

Beverage:  Milk 1983

Colors:  Colonial blue and buff

# HISTORY

In 1631 a settlement was attempted by the Dutch near Lewes but it was destroyed by the Indians.

The first successful colony was made by the Swedes in 1638 at Fort Christina now known as Wilmington. This colony was called New Sweden.

In 1655 New Sweden was invaded and captured by the Dutch.

The Dutch were conquered by the British in 1664.

William Penn was granted part of the territory in 1682.

In 1776, the district unit called the Three Lower Counties broke off from William Penn's territory to form the state of Delaware.

Delaware was the first state to ratify the Constitution. The state of Delaware ratified the Constitution on December 7, 1787.

Despite being a slave state Delaware remained in the Union during the Civil War (1861-1865).

The whipping post was abolished as a form of punishment in 1972.

# FACTS AND TRIVIA

Delaware is called the Blue Hen State. This dates back to the Revolutionary War when soldiers enjoyed pitting their blue hen chickens in cockfights. Delaware men were noted for their bravery and valor and compared to these fighting cocks.

More than 1/2 of the Fortune 500 companies have incorporated in Delaware. It was called the corporate state in 1973 because of its liberal incorporation laws.

There is no National Park System in Delaware. Delaware is the only state without any national historic sites, parks, battlefields, monuments or memorials.

In May, Delaware's shore displays large numbers of horseshoe crabs. These horseshoe crabs have remained basically unchanged since the dinosaur age and they can actually go for a year without eating.

Seaford, Delaware is called the Nylon Capital of the World. Nylon was first produced by Du Pont Laboratories at the Du Pont Seaford plant.

Barratts Chapel in Frederica, Delaware is where the Methodist Church of America was organized in 1784 . The Chapel was built in 1780.

Thomas Garret a Quaker merchant and famed abolitionist is thought to be the model for the novel *Uncle Toms Cabin*. His entire fortune was lost in legal proceedings involving fines for aiding a black family in a fight. Garrets role in the Underground Railroad aided more than 2,000 fugitive slaves through Delaware.

Delaware is only 1/2 the size of Los Angeles County. It ranks 49th in total land area with only 2,044 square miles including 112 square miles of inland water. It is from 9 to 35 miles wide and is 96 miles long.

Dover, Delaware is the boyhood home of John Dickinson. Dickinson was known as the Penman of the Revolution because of his writings on independence.

# FLORIDA

Florida:  Florida was named by Ponce de Leon for the Easter festival of flowers which is called *Pascua Florida*.

Capital:  Tallahassee

Flower:  Orange blossom (*Citrus sinensis*) 1909

Wildflower:  Coreopsis 1991

Tree:  Sabal palm or cabbage palmetto palm (*Sabal palmetto*) 1953

Bird:  Mockingbird (*Mimus polyglottos*) 1927

Nickname:  The Sunshine State

Rank:  27 (March 3, 1845)

Motto:  In God We Trust

Song:  Swanee River (The Old Folks At Home) by Stephen C. Foster 1935

Band:  St. Johns River City Band 1990

Fiddle Contest:  White Springs, Florida 1989

Gem:  Moonstone   Commemorates the Kennedy Space Center and the United States July 20, 1969 moon landing.  1970

Stone:  Agatized coral 1979

Shell:  Horse conch (*Pleuroploca gigantea*) 1969

Soil:  Myakka fine sand 1989

Animal:  Florida panther (*Felis concolor coryi*), endangered 1982

Butterfly:  Zebra long wing butterfly (*Heliconius charitonius*) 1996

Reptile:  American alligator (*Alligator mississippiensis*), controlled management 1987

Marine Mammal:  Manatee or sea cow (*Sirenia*) or Florida manatee (*Trichechus manatus*), endangered 1975

Saltwater Mammal:  Porpoise or bottle-nosed dolphin (*Tursiops truncatus*) 1975

Saltwater Fish:  Atlantic sailfish (*Istiophorus platypterus*) 1975

Freshwater Fish:  Florida largemouth bass (*Micropterus salmoides floridanus*) 1975

Beverage:  Orange juice 1967

Play: *Cross and Sword* by Paul Green 1973

Litter Control Symbol:  Keep Florida Beautiful

Pascua Week:  March 27-April 2

Florida Day:  The 2nd day of April  This is the date it is thought Ponce de Leon first sighted Florida in 1513.  1953

Fair:  Central Florida Air Fair

Festival:  Calle Ocho Open House 8

Pageant:  Indian River in Brevard County

Rodeo:  Silver Spurs Rodeo in Osceola County

# HISTORY

Juan Ponce de Leon claimed Florida for Spain in 1534.

Florida was claimed for France in 1562.

Fort Caroline was built by the French on the St. Johns River in 1564.

In 1565 the Fort Caroline settlement was destroyed by the Spanish.

Pedro Menendez founded the first permanent white settlement at St. Augustine.

Spain ceded Florida to England in 1763 but England gave the region back to Spain. Spain sold Florida to the U. S. in 1819 for five million dollars.

The Seminole Indian War lasted from 1835-1842.

Florida ceded from the Union in 1861 and was readmitted in 1868.

Miami Beach was developed as a resort by Carl Fisher in 1912.

In 1980 more than 100,000 Cuban refugees entered the United States. Most of these refugees entered through Florida.

Lake Kissimmee River was allowed to canalize in 1971.

The largest lake in Florida, Lake Okeechobee was returned to its natural course in 1990. Florida is just above sea level and has many lakes and swamps.

# FACTS AND TRIVIA

Over the last twenty years the climate in Florida attracts many retirees and millions of tourist each year. Palm Beach, Cypress Gardens and Disney World are primary tourist attractions for Florida.

Space flights are launched from Cape Canaveral.

The most visited amusement park in the United States is Walt Disney World / EPCOT Center in Orlando, Florida.

One of the 2 naturally round lakes in the world is in DeFuniak Springs.

Fort Lauderdale is called the Venice of America because it has 185 miles of local waterways.

The Boogy Bayou Mullet Festival is held the third weekend in October in Niceville.

On February 19, 1999 the world's largest strawberry shortcake was made in Plant City, Florida. The cake weighed 6,000 pounds and was made in McCall Park.

The Sports Fishing Capital of the world is in Islamorada, the Dive Capital is in Key Largo and the Shark Tooth Capital is in Venice.

Benwood is the most dived shipwreck in the world. It is in the Florida Keys on French Reef.

Suntan cream was invented in 1944 by pharmacist Benjamin Green in Miami Beach.

The U. S. city with the highest average temperature is Key West.

In 1539 explorer Hernando de Sota discovered Espiritu Santo Springs while he was searching for the Fountain of Youth. The natural springs have curative powers and are in Safety Harbor, Florida.

The first bank automated teller machine for roller bladers was installed in Miami.

# GEORGIA

Georgia:  The state of Georgia was named for King George II of England in 1732.

Capital:  Atlanta

Flower:  Cherokee rose (*Rosa laevigata*) 1916

Wildflower:  Azalea 1979

Tree:  Live oak (*Quercus virginiana*) 1937

Bird:  Brown thrasher (*Toxostoma rufum*) 1935 and 1970

Game Bird:  Bobwhite quail (*Colinus virginianus*) 1970

Nickname:  The Peach State or The Empire State of the South

Rank:  4 (January 2, 1788)

Motto:  Wisdom, justice and moderation

Creed:  Georgia Creed 1939

Song:  Georgia On My Mind by Stuart Gorrel and Hoagy Carmichael 1979

Waltz:  Our Georgia by James Burch 1951

Folk Dance:  Square dance

Gem:  Quartz (amethyst and clear quartz) 1976

Mineral:  Staurolite (fairy crosses or stones) 1976

Fossil:  Shark tooth, Tertiary 1976

Insect:  Honeybee (*Apis mellifera*) 1975

Butterfly:  Tiger swallowtail butterfly (*Papilio glaucus*) 1988

Reptile:  Gopher tortoise (*Gopherus polyphemus*) 1989

Marine Mammal:  Right whale (*Eubabalena glacialis*), endangered 1985

Fish:  Largemouth bass (*Micropterus salmoides*) 1970

Seashell:  Knobbed or Keiner's whelk (*Busycon carica eliceans*) 1987

Fruit:  Peach 1995

Crop:  Peanut 1995

Vegetable:  Vidalia sweet onion 1990

Peanut Monument:  Ashburn, Georgia

Art Museum:  Georgia Museum of Art in Athens, Georgia 1982

Railroad Museum:  Georgia Railroad Shops Central in Savannah

Poultry Capital of the World:  Georgia

Theater:  The Springer Opera House 1992

Musical Theater:  Jekyll Island Musical Theater Festival

Historic Drama:  *The Reach of Song* 1990

Folk Life Play:  *Swamp Gravy*

Folk Festival:  Georgia Folk Festival 1992

Beef Cook-off:  Shoot the Bull Barbecue in Hawkinsville, Georgia

Pork Cook-off:  Slosheye Trail Big Pig Jig in Vienna, Georgia

Possum:  "*Pogo*" Possum by Walt Kelly 1992

Atlas:  Atlas of Georgia 1985

Poet Laureate:  David Bottoms 2000-2004

High School:  Plains High School

# HISTORY

Cherokee Indians lived in the highlands and Creek Indians lived in the lowlands before white settlers came.

In 1540 the region was explored by Hernando de Soto.

The region was claimed by the English in 1629 as part of the Carolina grant made by King Charles I. General James Oglethorpe and his group of poor and religiously persecuted Englishmen were deeded the land by King George II in 1732. He brought the first settlers to the Savannah area in 1733.

In 1742 the Spanish were defeated at Bloody Marsh by Oglethorpe.

Georgia sent munitions to the Continental Army and fought with British troops led by Cornwallis evacuating the British from Savannah in 1782.

The Creek Indian tribes were deported from the state in 1832 followed by the Cherokee Indian tribes in 1838. The Trail of Tears lasted from 1832-1838.

Georgia seceded from the Union in 1861.

General William T. Sherman made his famous "March to the Sea". His 60,000 troops burned Atlanta and cut a 60 mile swathe to the sea in 1864. The path made by this Civil War march is still visible from the air.

In 1886 Coca Cola was invented by a Georgia chemist who was trying to find the cure for a hangover. Dr. Pepper was also invented in Georgia.

Georgia was the first state to give voting rights to 18 year olds in 1948.

A 100 million dollar philanthropic gift was given to Emory University by Robert W. Woodruff in 1979.

The state of Georgia was found in violation of the 1965 Voting Rights Act in its process for electing superior court judges by the Department of Justice in 1990.

# FACTS AND TRIVIA

President James Earl Carter and Rosalyn Carter were both graduates of Plains High School. The official state school of Georgia is Plains High School.

Thomasville, Georgia is called the City of Roses.

Six Flags over Georgia theme park was named for the six flags which have flown over Georgia.

The second oldest city in the nation is Saint Marys.

Stone Mountain is the site of the largest sculpture in the world. Jefferson Davis, Stonewall Jackson, Robert E. Lee and his horse Traveler are sculpted on the granite face of Stone Mountain.

Augusta hosts the annual Masters Golf Tournament at Augusta National.

Martha Berry Highway (US 27) extends the length of Georgia. She was a pioneer educator. Berry college in Rome is the world's largest college campus.

Georgia is host to the largest poultry convention in the world or the International Poultry Trade Show. Georgia is also Quail Capital of the World.

The Watermelon Capital of the World is Cordele, Georgia.

Okefenokee swamp provides sanctuaries for many species of wildlife and birds. The swamp encompasses over 400,000 acres. Okefenokee is an Indian word which means the trembling earth.

# HAWAII

Hawaii: The name Hawaii is thought to have originated from *Hawaiki*, the traditional Polynesian homeland or from *Hawaii Loa* the traditional discoverer of islands.

Capital: Honolulu

Flower: Native yellow hibiscus, mao-hau-hele or pua aloalo (*Hibiscus brackenridgei*) 1923 and 1988

Tree: Candlenut tree or *kukui* (*Aleurites moluccana*) 1959

Bird: Hawaiian goose or *nene* (*Branta sandvicensis*) 1988

Nickname: The Aloha State

Rank: 50 (August 21, 1959)

Motto: *Ua mau ke ea o ka aina i ka pono* (The life of the land is perpetuated in righteousness) The motto is attributed to King Kamehameha III. 1843

Song: Hawai i Pono i (Anthem) by King Kalakaua and Henry Berger 1967

Dance: Hula 1999

Gem: Black coral (*Antipathes grandis*) 1987

Marine Mammel: Humpback whale (*Megaptera novaeangliae*) 1979

Fish: *Humuhumunukunukuapua'a*, Hawaiian trigger fish or rectangular trigger fish (*Rhinecanthus rectanglus*) 1985

Individual Sport: Surfing 1998

Team Sport: Outrigger canoe paddling 1986

Native Language: Hawaiian 1978

# HISTORY

The first Polynesians arrived to inhabit Hawaii in the 6th century.

In the 10th century another group of Polynesians came to the islands.

The first European to explore Hawaii was Captain James Cook in 1778. He was killed on the island while attempting to retrieve a stolen boat in 1779.

Land reform ended the feudal system in 1848.

In 1893 a revolt by sugar cane and pineapple growers ended Monarchy rule and the Hawaiian Republic was established under Sanford B. Dole.

The Hawaii Islands were organized as a territory in 1900.

World War II began when Japanese attacked Pearl Harbor in 1941.

## FACTS AND TRIVIA

There are 8 major islands in Hawaii. They are Hawaii, Maui, Molokai, Kahoolawe, Lanai, Oahu, Kauai and Niihau. These are divided into the four counties of Maui, Hawaii, Kauai and Honolulu.

The Hawaiian alphabet has only 12 letters. The alphabet contains all of the English vowels (A, E, I, O and U) but only includes 7 English consonants (H, K, L, M, N, P and W).

Volcanoes which erupted thousands of years ago created Hawaii. The biggest mountain range in the world is the Hawaiian Islands.

Measured from it's base at the ocean floor Mauna Kea is the tallest mountain in the world. The most active volcano in the world is Kilauea. It has been in continuous eruption since 1983. The largest volcano in the world is Mauna Loa. Volcanoes National Park is on the island of Hawaii.

Hawaii grows one third of the worlds commercial supply of pineapples.

The 69 square mile island of Niihau is privately owned. General public access is limited and livestock raising is the islands principal industry.

Honolulu is on the island of Oahu. It is the largest city in the world. Honolulu is approximately 1,500 miles long.

There are more than 100 world renowned beaches in Honolulu.

Haleakala National Park is on the island of Maui. The largest dormant volcano in the world is the Haleakaia Crater.

The largest sea cliffs in the world are on the island of Molokai.

One of the best diving spots in the world is Hulope Bay on Lanai.

The island of Kahoolawe is 45 square miles of uninhabited area. It was once used for target practice by the military. The United States Air Force and Navy are still cleaning up unexploded shells.

The average temperature in Hawaii is between 72 and 82 degrees.

Hibiscus blossoms come in thousands of colors and combinations of colors. The Hawaiian hibiscuses were probably crossed with the hibiscuses from China. Each of the 8 islands are represented by the following colored hibiscus: Niihau (white), Kauai (purple), Oahu (yellow), Hawaii (red), Maui (pink), Molokai (green), Kahoolawe (gray) and Lanai (yellow).

Kalaaupapa on Molokai was once a leper colony administered by Father Damien.

# IDAHO

Idaho:  The word *Idaho* means gem of the mountains.
Capital:  Boise
Flower:  Syringa or mock orange (*Philadelphus lewisii*) 1931
Tree:  Western white pine (*Pinus monticola pinaceac*) 1935
Bird:  Mountain bluebird (*Sialia arctcia*) 1931
Nickname:  The Gem State or The Land of Famous Potatoes
Rank:  43 (July 3, 1890)
Motto:  *Esto Perpetua* (Let it be perpetual)
Song:  Here We Have Idaho (University of Idaho alma mater) by
       McKinley Helm, Albert J. Tompkins and Sallie Hume
       Douglas 1931
Folk Dance:  Square dance 1989
Gemstone:  Star garnet 1967
Fossil:  Hagerman horse fossil (*Equus simplicidens or Plesippus
       shoshonensis*), Pliocene 1988
Horse:  Appaloosa (*Equus caballus*) 1975
Insect:  Monarch butterfly (*Danaus plexippus*) 1992
Fish:  Cutthroat trout (*Oncorhynchus clarki*) 1990

# HISTORY

The area was explored by Meriwether Lewis and William Clark in 1805.

In the Idaho Treaty of 1846 Britain ceded the region to the United States.

Gold was discovered near Lewiston in 1859. The gold rush in 1860 brought many new settlers including the Mormons who settled in Franklin.

Idaho was organized into a territory in 1863.

Indian wars broke out in 1877 and many soldiers and settlers were killed. Chief Joseph and the Nez Perce tribe attempted to escape to Canada. They were pursued by troops for 1,300 miles but captured before reaching the border.

In 1951 Idaho Falls became the site of the worlds first breeder reactor.

Lewiston became linked to the Pacific Ocean at Actoria when the Snake River was opened to navigation in 1975.

In 1976 the new Teton River Dam collapsed when it was being filled for the first time. There was 400 million dollars in damage and 10 people killed.

# FACTS AND TRIVIA

Idaho has five wilderness areas and four national forest. It is second only to Alaska in designated wilderness area. There are over 5 1/2 million acres of designated wilderness area in Idaho.

From Heavens Gate Lookout at Seven Devils Peaks you can actually see four states.

The world famous Lava Hot Springs are in Idaho.

There are more than 2,000 lakes in Idaho. Lake Pend Oreille is the largest covering 180 square miles.

In Blackfoot, Idaho the eastern Idaho State Fair is held.

The Appaloosa horse was first bred to be used as a war animal in the Kamiah Valley by ancestors of the legendary Nez Perce Indian tribe.

Hells Canyon in Idaho is the deepest gorge in north America.

In 1907 President Theodore Roosevelt created the Caribou National Forest. The forest now consists of over one million acres.

Soda Springs has the largest man made geyser in the world.

Sawtooth National Recreational Area was named for the jagged profile of the mountain named Sawtooth Mountain.

Yellowstone National Park is in Idaho, Wyoming and Montana.

The largest tree in the state of Idaho is in Elk River. The Idaho Champion Western Red Cedar tree is 18 feet in diameter and 177 feet tall. The tree is estimated to be over 3,000 years old.

Since 1927 Shelley has hosted the Idaho Annual Spud Day.

The National Old Time Fiddlers Contest is held in Weiser.

When the American Falls Dam was first built in the mid 1920's the entire town of American Falls had to be relocated.

The nations longest highway through a national forest is the Lewis and Clark Highway (US 12).

Shoshone Falls near Twin Falls is called the Niagara of the West. The falls spills over 212 feet.

# ILLINOIS

Illinois:  Illinois is derived from early natives of the region or *iliniwek*
which means tribe of the superior men.

Capital:  Springfield

Flower:  Native blue violet or door yard violet (*Viola sororia*) 1908

Tree:  White oak (*Quercus alba*) 1973

Bird:  Cardinal (*Cardinalis cardinalis*) 1929

Nickname:  The Prairie State

Rank:  21 (December 3, 1818)

Motto:  State sovereignty--national union

Song:  Illinois by C. H. Chamberlain and Archibald Johnston 1925

Folk Dance:  Square dance 1990

Mineral:  Fluorite or calcium fluoride (*CaF2*) 1965

Fossil:  Tully Monster (*Tullimonstrum gregarium*), Pennsylvanian 1989

Prairie Grass:  Big bluestem (*Andropogon gerardii*) 1989

Animal:  White tailed deer (*Odocoileus virginianus*) 1982

Insect:  Monarch butterfly (*Danaus plexippus*) 1975

Fish:  Bluegill (*Lepomis macrochirus*) 1986

Slogan:  Land of Lincoln 1955

# HISTORY

French missionaries Jacques Marquette and Louis Jolliet explored the region in 1673.

Rene Robert Cavelier de La Salle built Fort Crevecoeur in 1680.

In 1692 Fort St. Louis became the first settlement.

The French ceded the territory to England in 1763 after the French and Indian War. In 1783 the British ceded the region to the United States.

Kaskaskia was taken from the British by George Rogers Clark in 1778.

Jean-Baptiste Point du Sable founded Chicago in 1778.

Indian tribes were defeated in the Black Hawk War of 1832.

The Mississippi River and Lake Michigan were linked by the Illinois and Michigan Canal in 1848.

In 1860 Springfield was the site of the Lincoln-Douglas Debates.

The great Chicago fire destroyed over half the city in 1871.

At the University of Chicago on December 2, 1942 Enrico Fermi and a small group of engineers and scientists constructed the first nuclear fission reactor in a squash court under the football stadium.

There were riots at the 1968 Democratic National Convention.

The tallest building in North America is the Sears Tower in Chicago, Illinois. The Sears Tower is 1,454 feet tall and was completed in 1973.

# FACTS AND TRIVIA

Lincoln's home is a national historic site and Lincoln's tomb is a state historic site. Both the home and tomb are in Springfield, Illinois.

In 1893 the first aquarium opened in Chicago.

The "Land of Lincoln" slogan was adopted in 1955 and appears on Illinois license plates. Illinois choose to recognize Abraham Lincoln for his humanity, statesmanship and as a symbol of democracy.

Illinois became the first state to abolish slavery in 1865.

Before Springfield was designated as capital of Illinois, Kaskaskia and Vandalia had both been designated as its capital.

The first McDonalds restaurant was located in Des Plaines.

In Decatur, Illinois the Staley Bears were organized in 1920. The Staley Bears are now known as the NFL's Chicago Bears.

Nauvoo is the site of the first Mormon Temple built in Illinois.

Superman really does have a home named Metropolis. Metropolis is located in southern Illinois.

In 1885 the 1st Skyscraper in the world was built in Chicago, Illinois.

The Chicago Board of Trade is the oldest and largest commodities exchange in the world.

At Grant Park in Chicago the Buckingham Fountain sprays columns of water in varied patterns and heights up to 135 feet.

The 300,000 acre Shawnee National Forest is located in Harrisburg.

In Oak Park the homes of Ernest Hemingway the writer and Frank Lloyd Wright the architect are both preserved as museums.

# INDIANA

Indiana:  The state was named by early settlers for the many distinct
             Indian tribes in the region.  Indiana means land of Indians.

Capital:  Indianapolis

Flower:  Peony (*Paeonie*) 1957

Tree:  Tulip tree or tulip poplar (*Liriodendron tulipifera*) 1931

Bird:  Cardinal (*Cardinalis cardinalis*) 1933

Nickname:  The Hoosier State

Rank:  19 (December 11, 1816)

Motto:  The Crossroads of America 1937

Song:  On The Banks Of The Wabash, Far Away by Paul Dresser 1913

Stone:  Limestone 1971

Fish:  Largemouth bass (*Micropterus salmoides*)

Poem:  *Indiana* by Arthur Franklin Mapes 1963

River:  The Wabash River 1996

# HISTORY

Potawatomi and Miami Indians inhabited the region when it was visited by French explorer Rene Robert Cavelier de La Salle in 1679-1687.

The first permanent settlement of the region was made by the French at Vincennes in 1732.

In 1763 the French ceded the region to the British.

The British were expelled from the region by General George Rogers Clark when American troops captured Fort Vincennes in 1779.

Britain ceded the territory to the United States in 1783. The region was organized into the Northwest Territory in 1787.

General Anthony Wayne defeated the Miami Indians in 1794 at the battle of Fallen Timbers.

Indiana Territory was divided from the Northwest Territory in 1800.

At the battle of Tippecanoe in 1811 General William Henry Harrison defeated the Tecumsehs Indian Confederation.

On May 30, 1911 the first long distance auto race in the United States was held at the Indianapolis Motor Speedway.

# FACTS AND TRIVIA

Indianapolis is home to the NBA Indiana Pacers basketball team and the NFL Indianapolis Colts football team.

The world headquarters of the Amateur Athletic Union (AAU) is in Indianapolis.

Parke County with its 32 covered bridges is the Covered Bridge Capital of the World.

Indiana Medical History Museum is in Indianapolis. It is the nations oldest surviving pathology laboratory. The museum displays over 15,000 artifacts and has 12 historic rooms.

Indianapolis Motor Speedway and Hall of Fame Museum in Indianapolis exhibits antique and classic passenger cars, one of a kind special interest race cars and 30 Indy 500 winning cars.

Lincoln Boyhood National Memorial in Spencer County is where Abraham Lincoln lived from 1816-1830.

Indianapolis is the base for many of the trucking lines in America because it is the junction for many interstate highways.

Indiana adopted the motto "Crossroads of America" because of its physical location. Since the days of wilderness explorers, Indiana has been a corridor for movement from north to south and east to west.

The National Track and Field Hall of Fame is in Indianapolis.

Montgomery County jail in Crawfordsville is the only working rotary jail in the United States. It is now a museum but served as the Montgomery County Jail from 1882-1972.

In 1871 the first professional baseball game was played in Fort Wayne.

Over one half million letters with requests to Santa are received by Santa Claus, Indiana each year.

# IOWA

Iowa:  The state was named for the *Iowa* Indian tribe.

Capital:  Des Moines

Flower:  Any wild rose or the wild prairie rose (*Rosa pratincola*) 1897

Tree:  Oak (*Quercus*) 1961

Bird:  American goldfinch (*Carduelis tristis*) 1933

Nickname:  The Hawkeye State

Rank:  29 (December 28, 1846)

Motto:  Our liberties we prize and our rights we will maintain

Song:  Song Of Iowa by S. H. M. Byers to the music of O'Tannenbaum by Lauriger Horatius 1911

Stone:  Geode 1967

Fish:  Channel catfish (*Ictalurus punctatus*), Unofficial*

## PROPOSED

Song:  Iowa Corn Song by George Hamilton

Folk Dance:  Square dance

Mammal:  Bison

Fossil:  Crinoid

Insect:  Honeybee and ladybug

Soil:  Tama soil

# HISTORY

The region was claimed for France by Jacques Marquette and Louis Jolliet in 1673.

In 1785 Julien Dubuque made the first settlement near the city that now bears his name.

The region was ceded to Spain in 1763 and returned to France in 1800. Land including Iowa was purchased by the United States from France as part of the Louisiana Purchase in 1803.

In 1812 land which included Iowa became part of the Missouri Territory. It became part of Michigan Territory in 1834 then part of Wisconsin Territory. In 1838 Iowa was established as a territory.

Iowa furnished nearly eighty thousand men to the Union Army during the Civil War. The state supported Abraham Lincoln and Republican ideology.

Des Moines replaced Iowa City as the state capital in 1857.

Fifty percent of the farmers in Iowa lost their farms during the depression which lasted from 1929-1935.

# FACTS AND TRIVIA

One forth of the nations richest and deepest topsoil is in Iowa. The highest percentage of grade A topsoil in the nation is in Wright County.

Cedar Rapids is home to Quaker Oats which is the largest cereal company in the world.

The National Balloon Museum is located in Indianola.

Dubuque is home to the Fenton Place Elevator which is the steepest and shortest railway in the world.

In Winnebago County, campers and motor homes are manufactured.

The largest collection of Grant Wood artwork is at the Cedar Rapids Museum of Art.

In Sioux City the Sergeant Floyd Monument honors the only man that died during the Lewis and Clark expedition.

The National Sprint Car Hall of Fame and Museum is in Knoxville.

John Wayne the actor was born in Winterset, Iowa on May 26, 1907. His real name was Marion Robert Morrison and he was the son of a pharmacist.

The Dubuque County courthouse is the only county courthouse with a gold dome.

Herbert Hoover National Historic Site is located west of Davenport and features the cottage where he was born. The Hoover Presidential Library Museum is also at this site.

The only fort ever built to protect one Indian tribe from another was in the town of Fort Atkinson.

Snake Alley in Burlington is called the crookedest street in the world.

Effigy Mounds National Monument is the site of 191 prehistoric Indian mounds. Twenty nine of these mounds are in the shape of animals and birds.

Kate Shelley Bridge in Boone is the highest double track railroad bridge in the world.

# KANSAS

Kansas:  The state was named after the *Kaw* or *Kansa* who were also known as people of the south wind.

Capital:  Topeka

Flower:  Wild native sunflower (*Helianthus annuus*) 1903

Tree:  Cottonwood (*Populus deltoides*) 1937

Bird:  Western meadowlark (*Sturnella neglecta*) 1937

Nickname:  The Sunflower State or The Jayhawk State

Rank:  34 (January 29, 1861)

Motto:  *Ad Astra per Aspera* (To the stars through difficulties)

Song:  Home On The Range by Dr. Brewster Higley and Daniel Kelly 1947

Marches:  Kansas March by Duff E. Middleton 1935
Here's Kansas by Bill Post 1992

Animal:  American buffalo (*Bison americanus*) 1955

Insect:  Honeybee (*Apis mellifera*) 1976

Reptile:  Ornate box turtle (*Terrapene ornata agassiz*) 1986

Amphibian:  Barred tiger salamander (*Ambystoma tigrium mavortium*) 1994

Fish:  Channel catfish (*Ictalurus punctatus*)

Banner:  Kansas banner 1925

# HISTORY

In 1540-1541 Francisco Vasquez de Coronado lead the first major expedition of the Kansas region.

The territory which included Kansas was claimed by Rene Robert Cavelier de La Salle in 1682 for France.

In 1803 the United States acquired the region as part of the Louisiana Purchase. In 1850 the southwestern part, which had been part of Texas, became part of the Missouri Territory.

Pioneers were protected on the Oregon and Santa Fe trails by Fort Leavenworth (1827), Fort Scott (1842) and Fort Riley (1853).

The Kansas Nebraska Act organized Kansas as a territory in 1854.

There was so much pre-war violence in Kansas over slavery issues from 1854-1856 it became known as "Bleeding Kansas".

Large areas of Kansas were devastated by Quantrill's raiders and other groups before the Confederacy was defeated in 1865.

The Menninger Foundation for mental health was founded in 1919.

Kansas suffered during the depression and during the Dust Bowl drought from 1934-1935.

# FACTS AND TRIVIA

Amelia Earhart was from Atchison, Kansas. She was the first woman to fly solo across the Atlantic Ocean and the first granted a pilots license by the National Aeronautics Association.

Susan Madora Salter of Kansas was the first woman mayor.

The Wheat Capital of the World is in Sumner County. There was enough wheat produced in Kansas in 1997 to make 35.9 billion loaves of bread.

Dwight D. Eisenhower was from Abilene, Kansas. He was the 34th President of the United States.

Meades Ranch is about 40 miles south of Lebanon, Kansas. When property is surveyed the surveyor is actually checking the position of the property in relation to Meades Ranch.

In Cawker City there is a ball of twine weighing more than 16,750 pounds. The ball of twine has a circumference of over 38 feet.

Barton County was named after Civil War nurse Clara Barton.

One of the richest salt deposits in the world is in Hutchinson, Kansas.

A horse named Comanche was the only 7th Cavalry survivor in the Battle of the Little Big Horn or Custer's last stand. The 7th Cavalry was formed at Fort Riley, which is just outside of Manhattan, by George Custer in 1866.

The largest natural gas field in the United States is the 8,500 square mile Hugoton Gas Field. The gas field underlies part of southwestern Kansas and parts of Oklahoma and Texas.

The governors mansion in Topeka, Kansas is called Cedar Crest.

Hattie McDaniel of Kansas was the first black woman to win an Academy Award for her role as Mammy in "*Gone with the Wind*".

The windiest city in the United States is Dodge City, Kansas.

# KENTUCKY

Kentucky:  The name is derived from Iroquois *kenta-ke* meaning meadow land or from Wyandot *kah-ten-tah-teh* meaning land of tomorrow.

Capital:  Frankford

Flower:  Goldenrod (*Solidago*) 1926

Tree:  Tulip poplar (*Liriodendron tulipifera*) 1994

Bird:  Cardinal (*Cardinalis cardinalis*) 1926

Nickname:  The Bluegrass State

Rank:  15 (June 1, 1792)

Motto:  United we stand, divided we fall

Song:  My Old Kentucky Home (modern version) by Stephen C. Foster 1986 and 1988

Bluegrass Song:  Blue Moon of Kentucky 1988

Pipe Band:  Louisville Pipe Band 2000

Gemstone:  Freshwater pearl 1986

Mineral:  Coal 1998

Rock:  Kentucky agate 2000

Fossil:  Brachiopod, Paleozoic 1986

Soil:  Crider soil series 1990

Wild Game Animal:  Gray squirrel (*Sciurus carolinensis*) 1968

Horse:  Thoroughbred (*Equus caballus*) 1996

Butterfly:  Viceroy butterfly (*Basilarchia archippus*) 1990

Fish:  Kentucky spotted bass (*Micropterus puctulatus*) 1956

Arboretum:  Bernheim Arboretum and Research Forest 1994

Silverware Pattern:  Old Kentucky Bluegrass (Georgetown pattern) 1996

Covered Bridge:  Switzer covered bridge in Franklin County 1998

Covered Bridge Capital:  Fleming County 1998

Tug of War Championship:  Fordsville in Ohio County 1990

Botanical Garden:  UK Arboretum 2000

Steam Locomotive:  *Old 152* 2000

# HISTORY

The region was first explored and claimed for France by Rene Robert Cavelier de La Salle from 1648-1687.

In 1750 the English attempted to settle and claim the region but were driven out by Indians.

The French ceded the region to Spain in 1762.

Pennsylvania settlers established the first permanent settlement of Kentucky at Harrodsburg in 1775. The British spurred Indian attacks.

Fort Boonesborough was founded by Daniel Boone in 1776.

The territory was organized in 1776 as a county of Virginia.

In 1783 after the Revolutionary War the region was ceded to the United States by the British.

Kentuckians joined in Andrew Jackson's campaign during the War of 1812 to defend New Orleans against the British.

In 1815 the first steamboat reached Louisville from New Orleans.

Confederate armies invaded the state in 1862. During the Civil War Kentucky was divided. The Bluegrass gentry supported the Confederacy and the Appalachian backwoods men supported the Union.

In 1875 the Kentucky Derby was first run at Louisville. The first Saturday in May the Kentucky Derby is held at Churchill Downs. The Kentucky Derby Museum is also located in Louisville. The finest thoroughbred race horses in the world are raised in Lexington, Kentucky.

## FACTS AND TRIVIA

Kentucky is noted for its coal, tobacco, horse breeding, bourbon and bluegrass music.

Corbin, Kentucky is the site of the first Kentucky Fried Chicken restaurant owned and operated by Colonel Sanders.

Kentucky's state tree from 1976-1994 was the Kentucky coffee tree.

McCreary County is the site of the first commercial oil well. It was built on the Cumberland River in 1819.

Mammoth Cave is the longest cave system in the world. Echo River is 360 feet below ground in Mammoth Cave. Some of the rooms in the cave are 200 feet in height and there are over 300 miles of explored passageways.

My Old Kentucky Home State Park is in Bardstown, Kentucky.

The oldest continuously operated steamboat on the Mississippi is the *Belle of Louisville*. The stern wheeler was built in 1914 and offers excursions on the Ohio River.

Bowling Green is where all Chevrolet Corvettes are manufactured.

Murray State University is the location of the Boy Scouts of America Scouting Museum.

Abraham Lincoln's birthplace is a national historic site preserved in marble and granite in Hodgenville, Kentucky. Both the President of the Union, Abraham Lincoln and the President of the Confederacy, Jefferson Davis were born in Kentucky.

# LOUISIANA

Louisiana:  The state was named in honor of King Louis XIV, King of France by French explorer Rene Robert Cavelier de La Salle.

Capital:  Baton Rouge

Flower:  Magnolia (*Magnolia grandiflora*) 1900

Wildflower:  Louisiana iris (*Giganticaerulea*) 1990

Tree:  Bald cypress (*Taxodium distichum*) 1963

Bird:  Brown pelican (*Pelecanus occidentalis*) 1900 and 1966

Nickname:  The Pelican State

Rank:  18 (April 30, 1812)

Motto:  Union, justice and confidence

Songs:  Give Me Louisiana by Doralise Fontane and Dr. John Croom 1970

You Are My Sunshine by Governor Jimmy Davis and Charles Mitchell 1977  Singing Governor Jimmy Davis (1899-2000) also acted in westerns and taught history and yodeling at a women's college.

March Song:  Louisiana My Home Sweet Home by Sammie McKenzie, Lou Lavoy and Castro Carazo 1952

Environmental Song:  Gifts Of The Earth by Frances LeBeau 1990

Instrument:  Diatonic or Cajun accordion 1990

Gemstone:  Agate 1976

Fossil:  Petrified palmwood (*Palmoxylon*), Oligocene 1976

Mammal:  Louisiana black bear (*Ursus americanus luteolus*), endangered 1992

Dog:  Catahoula leopard dog (*Canis lupis familiaris*) 1979

Insect:  Honeybee (*Apis mellifera*) 1977

Amphibian:  Green tree frog (*Hyla cinerea*) 1993

Crustacean:  Crawfish or crayfish 1983

Freshwater Fish:  White perch, sac-au-lait or white crappie (*Pomoxis annularis*) 1993

Reptile:  Alligator (*Alligator mississippiensis*), threatened 1983

Drink:  Milk 1983

Colors:  Blue, white and gold 1972

Painting:  Louisiana by Johnny O. Bell and Johnny F. Bell 1995

Pledge of Allegiance:  Louisiana state flag pledge

Mardi Gras:  The annual celebration begins two weeks before Fat Tuesday which is the day before Lent.

# HISTORY

Hernando de Soto explored and claimed the region for Spain in 1541.

In 1682 Louisiana was claimed for France by Rene Robert Cavelier de La Salle along with Missouri and Mississippi which were also called Louisiana.

Natchitoches was the first settlement of present Louisiana in 1714.

New Orleans was founded by Bienville in 1718.

In 1755 more than 4,000 French settlers in Nova Scotia, Canada were forcibly transported by the British to Louisiana. They were resettled in Bayou Teche. This group of French settlers were called Acadians and their descendants are known as Cajuns. The Acadians were resettled because they would not pledge allegiance to the King of England.

The region was ceded to Spain in 1762 but returned to France in 1800.

A Spanish governor brought the Islenos to Louisiana in 1779. The Islenos were descendants of Canary Islanders.

Napoleon sold Louisiana to the United States on April 30, 1803. The land sold for about four cents an acre which amounted to 15 million dollars.

Confederate forces captured New Orleans in 1862. It was occupied until the war ended in 1877.

The Louisiana Creoles are descendants of French and Spanish settlers.

Local dialects in Louisiana reflect both French and Spanish heritage.

Petroleum was discovered in Louisiana in 1901.

# FACTS AND TRIVIA

The longest over water bridge in the world is the Causeway Bridge over Lake Pontchartrain. The Causeway Bridge is 24 miles long.

Hodges Gardens is a 4,700 acre horticultural park and wildlife refuge.

The state capital building in Louisiana has 34 floors and is 450 feet tall. It is the tallest state capitol building in the United States.

Baton Rouge is French for "red stick".

The largest domed structure in the United States is the Superdome in New Orleans, Louisiana.

New Orleans Museum of Art has a large jeweled Faberge exhibit.

The famous Battle of New Orleans was actually fought two weeks after the War of 1812 had ended.

All the counties in Louisiana are called parishes.

The Mardi Gras celebration in New Orleans, Louisiana is world famous.

Governor Huey Long struck what is called the "Devils Bargain" with the petrochemical industry. He was assassinated in 1935.

Texas is the only state with more oil and gas reserves than Louisiana.

The French Quarter is in New Orleans, Louisiana. Bourbon Street, the French Market, Jackson Square and Preservation Hall are located in the French Quarter.

On the first Friday after Easter the Spring Fiesta begins in New Orleans. During the Spring Fiesta many of the antebellum mansions from Jackson Avenue to Louisiana Avenue are open to the public.

# MAINE

Maine:  Maine is thought to be named after Maine in France or to distinguish mainland from islands in the Gulf of Maine.

Capital:  Augusta

Floral Emblem:  White pine cone and tassel (*Pinus strobus linnaeus*) 1895

Tree:  White pine (*Pinus strobus*) 1945 and 1975

Bird:  Chickadee (*Parus atricapillus*) 1927

Nickname:  The Pine Tree State

Rank:  23 (March 15, 1820)

Motto:  *Dirigo* (I direct)

Song:  State Of Maine Song by Roger Vinton Snow

Mineral:  Tourmaline 1971

Fossil:  Vascular land plant (*Pertica quadrifaria*), Devonian 1985

Soil:  Chesuncook soil series 1999

Animal:  Moose (*Alces alces*) 1979

Cat:  Maine coon cat (*Felis catus*) 1985

Insect:  Honeybee (*Apis mellifera*) 1975

Fish:  Landlocked or sebago salmon (*Salmo salar sebago*) 1969

Berry:  Wild blueberry (*Vaccinium angustifolium aiton*) 1991

Herb:  Wintergreen (*Gaultheria procumbens*) 1999

Vessel:  *Schooner Bowdoin* 1987

Language of the Deaf:  American sign language 1991

Tartan:  Maine State Tartan

# HISTORY

Maine was first settled by the French in 1604 at the St. Croix River. English settlers arrived in 1607 and settled on the Kennebec River.

Massachusetts governed Maine from 1691 to 1820.

During the Revolutionary War a British fleet destroyed Falmouth in 1775. Falmouth is now known as Portland.

On March 15, 1820 Maine separated from Massachusetts and was admitted to the Union.

Maine's border dispute with Canada was settled in 1842 by the terms of the Ashburton Treaty.

Prohibition law was enacted in 1851.

In 1980 the Passamaquoddy and Penobscot tribes settled their claims against the state for seized land. Claims were settled for 81 million dollars.

## FACTS AND TRIVIA

Maine is internationally famous for its lobsters. There are about 40 million pounds of lobsters caught off the coast of Maine each year. This accounts for approximately 90% of the lobsters harvested.

In 1641 York, Maine became America's first chartered city.

Portland was the first state capital of Maine. Augusta was designated as state capital in 1832.

The most easterly point in the United States is West Quoddy Head.

Maine has the largest blueberry crop in the nation and it produces 98% of the low bush blueberries in the nation.

In 1623 the first sawmill was established in York, Maine.

Henry Wadsworth Longfellow the poet was born in Portland, Maine on February 2, 1807. Longfellow House is in Portland which is where he spent his childhood. His most noted works include: Evangeline, Hiawatha and The Courtship of Miles Standish.

The most eastern capital city in the United States is Augusta, Maine.

Mt. Katahdin is 5,268 feet or just under one mile high. It is located in the Baxter State Park.

Penobscot Marine Museum is in Searsport, Maine. The Museum displays models of ships, whaling memorabilia and nautical charts.

Maine produces 90% of the toothpicks in the country.

Fort Knox is a state historic site in Maine. It was built in 1844 to protect the Penobscot River Valley from British naval attack. Granite from Mount Waldo was used to construct the fort.

The most eastern city in the United States is Eastport, Maine.

Maine's State Tartan was designed by Sol Gillis in 1964. It was first woven in 1988 by Jane Holmes of Plymouth. Her company the Maine Tartan and Tweed Company makes and sells items made from the fabric.

There is a cannery in Wilton, Maine that cans dandelion greens.

The second most visited national park in the United States is Acadia National Park in Maine.

# MARYLAND

Maryland:  The state of Maryland is named for Henrietta Maria the queen consort of King Charles I.

Capital:  Annapolis

Flower:  Black eyed susan (*Rudbeckia hirta*) 1918

Tree:  White oak (*Quercus alba*) 1941

Bird:  Baltimore oriole (*Ictercus galbula*) 1947

Nickname:  The Old Line State, The Free State, The Pine Tree State or The Lumber State

Rank:  7 (April 28, 1788)

Motto:  *Fatti Maschii, Parole Femine* (Manly deeds, womanly words)

Song:  Maryland, My Maryland by James Ryder Randall to the music of O'Tannanbaum by Lauriger Horatius 1939

Folk Dance:  Square dance 1994

Fossil Shell:  Extinct marine snail (*Ecphora gardnerae gardnerae*), Miocene 1994

Dinosaur:  Herbivorous sauropod (*Astrodon johnstoni*), Cretaceous 1998

Dog:  Chesapeake bay retriever (*Canis lupis familiaris*) 1964

Insect:  Baltimore checker spot butterfly (*Euphydryas phaeton*) 1973

Reptile:  Diamondback terrapin saltwater turtle (*Malaclemys terrapin*) 1994

Crustacean:  Blue crab (*Callinectes sapidus*) 1989

Fish:  Striped bass or rockfish (*Roccus saxatilis or Morone saxatilis*) 1965

Drink:  Milk 1998

Boat:  Skipjack 1985

Sport:  Jousting 1962

Theater:  Center Stage in Baltimore, Maryland 1978

Summer Theater:  Olney Theatre in Montgomery County 1978

# HISTORY

John Smith explored the area in 1608.

Kent Island trading post in Chesapeake Bay was set up by William Claiborne in 1631.

Cecilius Calvert, first Lord Baltimore was granted the land by King Charles I of Great Britain in 1632 to provide a refuge for people of the Catholic religion who were being persecuted.

Saint Marys was founded by 200 Catholic settlers and Leonard Calvert in 1634. There was dissidence among settlers of different religious groups.

Maryland was converted to a royal colony in 1692 by the King of England who put himself directly in charge of the colony.

The Baltimores regained the colony of Maryland in 1715.

In 1730 Baltimore was founded.

The Star Spangled Banner was written by Francis Scott Key on September 14, 1814 while the British were bombing Ft. McHenry in Baltimore Harbor. The Star Spangled Banner later became the National Anthem.

During the Civil War from 1861-1865 the state of Maryland was under federal military control.

In 1902 workmens compensation laws were first enacted in Maryland.

The first state to adopt income tax was Maryland in 1938.

While campaigning in the democratic presidential primary in 1972 Governor George C. Wallace of Alabama was shot in Maryland.

# FACTS AND TRIVIA

By joint Resolution of Congress since 1949 the United States flag has flown continuously over the monument marking the birthplace of Francis Scott Key in Keymar, Maryland.

The first dental school in the U. S. was at the University of Maryland.

In 1845 the United States Naval Academy was founded at Annapolis.

The capital of the United States was once Annapolis. Washington D. C. was originally part of Maryland. The state of Maryland gave up some of its land to create the capital.

St. Clare Station is the oldest railroad station in the United States.

The oldest state capital in continuous use is the Maryland State House.

Babe Ruth Birthplace Museum is in Baltimore, Maryland. The major league baseball player Babe Ruth was called "Sultan of Swat" or "The Babe".

Gaithersburg is called the Science Capital of the United States.

Saint Michaels is known as the town that fooled the British. On August 10, 1813 the town was warned of a British attack. The residents prepared for the attack by hoisting lanterns to the tops of trees and to the masts of ships. British cannons over shot the town.

The National Aquarium is in Baltimore, Maryland.

Maryland is a national leader in blue crab and soft clam production.

The first cathedral in the United States was the Basilica of the Assumption of the Blessed Virgin Mary in Baltimore, Maryland.

# MASSACHUSETTS

Massachusetts:  The state was named for the Massachuset Indian tribe. *Massachuset* means at or about the great hill.

Capital:  Boston

Flower:  Mayflower or ground laurel (*Epigaea regens*) 1918

Tree:  American elm (*Ulmus americana*) 1941

Bird:  Black capped chickadee (*Penthestes atricapillus*) 1941

Game Bird:  Wild turkey (*Meleagris gallopavo*) 1991

Nickname:  The Bay State, The Old Bay State, The Old Colony, The Puritan State or The Baked Bean State

Rank:  6 (February 6, 1788)

Motto:  *Ense Petit Placidam Sub Libertate Quietem* (By the sword we seek peace, but peace only under liberty)

Song:  All Hail To Massachusetts by Arthur J. Marsh 1981

Polka:  Say Hello To Someone In Massachusetts by Lenny Gomulka 1998

Ceremonial March Song:  The Road To Boston 1985

Folk Song:  Massachusetts by Arlo Guthrie 1981

Glee Club Song:  The Great State Of Massachusetts by George A. Wells and J. Earl Bley 1997

Patriotic Song:  Massachusetts (Because Of You Our Land Is Free) by Bernard Davidson 1990

Folk Dance:  Square dance 1990

Gem:  Rhodonite 1979

Mineral:  Babingtonite 1971

Rock:  Roxbury puddingstone or jasper 1983

Historical Rock:  Plymouth Rock 1983

Explorer Rock:  Dighton Rock 1983

Building and Monument Stone:  Granite 1983

Shell:  New England neptune (*Neptuna lyrata decemcostata*) 1987

Fossil:  Dinosaur tracks or theropod dinosaur prints, Triassic 1980

Soil:  Paxton soil series 1990

Dog:  Boston terrier (*Canis lupis familiaris bostenenis*) 1979

Cat:  Tabby cat (*Felis catus*) 1988

Horse:  Morgan horse (*Equus cabullus morganensis*) 1970

Insect:  Ladybug or two spotted lady beetle (*Adalia bipunctata*) 1974

Marine Mammal:  Right whale (*Eubabalena glacialis*) 1980

Fish:  Atlantic cod (*Gadus morhua*) 1974

Beverage:  Cranberry juice 1970

Berry:  Cranberry (*Vaccinium macrocarpon*) 1994

Bean:  Navy bean 1993

Muffin:  Corn muffin 1986

Dessert:  Boston cream pie 1996

Cookie:  Chocolate chip cookie 1997

Folk Hero: John Chapman or Johnny Appleseed   He planted apple seeds
in the state. 1996
Heroine: Deborah Samson   She fought in the War of Independence
under the name of Robert Shurtleff. 1983.
Poem: *Blue Hills of Massachusetts* by Katherine E. Mullen 1981
Citizenry: Bay Staters 1990

# HISTORY

In 1620 seeking religious freedom the Separatists or Pilgrims settled at
Plymouth.  Plymouth Rock marks the Pilgrims landing of the Mayflower.

The first Thanksgiving was held in 1621.

In 1636 Harvard, the first college in North America was founded.

The Boston Massacre was set off by demonstrations against British
restrictions on March 5, 1770.  British soldiers fired into a crowd of colonists.

In protest of taxation the Boston Tea Party was held on December 16,
1773.  Disguised as Indians, colonists boarded the Brig Beaver II and dumped
British tea into the harbor.  There is a replica of this ship at the Boston Tea
Party Ship and Museum in Boston.

The British marched on Lexington and Concord in 1775.

George Washington took command of the Continental Army in 1775.

Irish immigrated to Massachusetts to flee famine in 1845.

Cape Cod canal was completed in 1914.

# FACTS AND TRIVIA

Witchcraft trials were held in colonial times in Salem, Massachusetts.
The Salem Witch Museum recalls the 1692 witchcraft hysteria.

Glaciers during the ice age formed the islands of Marthas Vineyard and
Nantucket.  In 1973 they symbolically voted to secede from the state.

Lowell is where the American Industrial Revolution began.  Lowell
National Historical Park commemorates the role of the town in the revolution.

Quincy, Massachusetts is the site of the first Dunkin Donuts.  The first
Howard Johnsons was also in Quincy.

In 1897 the first subway system in the United States was built in Boston,
Massachusetts.

Springfield is the site of the Basketball Hall of Fame.  In 1891 the first
basketball game was played in Springfield.

Four United States presidents were born in Norfolk county.  They include;
John Adams, John Quincy Adams, John Fitzgerald Kennedy and George
Herbert Walker Bush.

In Rockport there is a house built exclusively of newspaper.  The house
was constructed by using 215 layers of newspaper.

The oldest ship in the United States Navy is the *USS Constitution*.  The
frigate was launched in 1797 and became known as "Old Ironsides".  The *USS
Constitution* is at the navy yard in Charlestown.

Clark University in Worcester, Massachusetts is where the birth control
pill was invented.

# MICHIGAN

Michigan: Michigan is derived from the Indian words *michi-gama* which means large lake.

Capital: Lansing

Flower: Apple blossom (*Pyrus coronaria*) 1897

Wildflower: Dwarf lake iris (*Iris lacustris*) 1998

Tree: White pine (*Pinus strobus*) 1955

Bird: Robin (*Turdus migratorius*) 1931

Nickname: The Great Lakes State, The Wolverine State or The Water Wonderland

Rank: 26 (January 26, 1837)

Motto: *Si Quaeris Peninsulam Amoenam Circumspice* (If you seek a pleasant peninsula, look about you)

Song: Michigan, My Michigan by William Otto Miessner and Douglas M. Malloch to the music of O'Tannenbaum by Lauriger Horatius 1937

Gem: Chlorastrolite, green star stone or Isle Royale greenstone 1972

Stone: Petoskey stone or fossilized coral (*Hexagonaria pericarnata*), Devonian 1965

Soil: Kalkaska soil series 1990

Game Mammal: White tailed deer (*Odocoileus virginianus*) 1997

Reptile: Painted turtle (*Chysemys picta*) 1995

Fish: Brook trout (*Salvelinus fontinalis*) 1988

Pledge of Allegiance: Michigan state flag pledge 1972

Coat of Arms: Michigan Coat of Arms 1911

# HISTORY

French fur traders and missionaries visited the region in 1616.

A mission was set up at Sault Sainte Marie in 1641 and in 1668 a settlement was founded by Father Jacques Marquette.

In 1701 Detroit was founded by the French as a military post.

After the French and Indian War the British controlled the region until the Treaty of Paris when it was ceded to the United States in 1783.

The British caused trouble for settlers by organizing Indian forces but they were defeated by General Anthony Wayne at Fallen Timbers in 1784.

In 1805 the region was organized into the Michigan Territory.

Michigan was the first state to outlaw capital punishment in 1846.

Jackson is where the Republican party was organized in 1854.

In 1896 both Henry Ford and Ransom E. Olds created gas powered cars.

The Detroit race riot in 1967 was one of the worst riots in U. S. history. There were 200 million dollars in damages and 43 people killed in the riot.

Michigan Public Act 165 of 1972 defined the pledge of allegiance to the Michigan state flag as follows: "I pledge allegiance to the flag of Michigan, and to the state for which it stands, 2 beautiful peninsulas united by a bridge of steel, where equal opportunity and justice to all is our ideal".

In 1979 the federal government authorized 1.5 billion dollars in loan guarantees to bail out the Chrysler Corporation.

# FACTS AND TRIVIA

Detroit, Michigan is the car capital of the world.

Incorporated in 1815, Wayne County is the oldest incorporated county.

The only place where you can find a petoskey stone is on the shores of Lake Michigan. The petoskey stone is Michigan's state stone.

Nationally Michigan ranks first in boat registrations.

The longest freshwater shoreline in the world is in Michigan.

Battle Creek, Michigan was made the Cereal Capital of the World by the Kellogg Company.

The largest registered Holstein dairy herd in the world is in Elsie.

There are 104 lighthouses in Michigan.

A good place to find the dwarf lake iris is among the sand dunes at Sleeping Bear Dunes National Lakeshore along the western shore of Michigan.

There are no more wolverines in Michigan.

The largest limestone quarry in the world is in Rogers City.

Gerald R. Ford was a native of Grand Rapids. He was an Eagle Scout, a football star for the University of Michigan, a Michigan congressman for 24 years and the 38th president of the United States.

Ranson E. Olds Transportation Museum is in Lansing.

The largest cement plant in the world is in Alpena, Michigan.

Henry Ford's estate is in Dearborn and it is called Fair Lane.

The largest crucifix in the world is called the "Cross in the Woods". The crucifix is in Indian River.

# MINNESOTA

Minnesota:  Minnesota is from the Sioux Indian word *minisota* which means sky tinted waters.

Capital:  St. Paul

Flower:  Pink and white lady slipper or showy lady slipper (*Cypripedium reginae*) 1893

Tree:  Red or Norway pine (*Pinus resinosa*) 1945 and 1953

Bird:  Loon (*Gavia immer*) 1961

Nickname:  The North Star State or The Gopher State

Rank:  32 (May 11, 1858)

Motto:  *L'etolie du Nord* (The star of the north) 1861

Song:  Hail! Minnesota (University of Minnesota alma mater) by Arthur E. Upson 1945

Gemstone:  Lake Superior agate 1969

Butterfly:  Monarch butterfly (*Danaus plexippus*) 2000

Fish:  Walleye (*Stizostedion vitreum vitreum*) 1965

Grain:  Wild rice (*Zizania aquatica*) 1977

Mushroom:  Morel (*Morchella esculenta*) 1984

Muffin:  Blueberry 1988

Drink:  Milk 1984

## PROPOSED OR FACETIOUS

Amphibian:  Northern leopard frog

Animal / Mammal:  Gopher (*Citelus tridecemlineatus*), White tailed deer (*Odocoileus virginianus borealis*) and Timber wolf (*Canis lupus*)

Beer:  Schell's Deer Brand and Cold Spring

Book:  *Little House on the Prairie*

Candy:  Licorice

Folk Dance:  Square dance

Fossil:  Giant beaver (*Castoroides ohioensis*) and Rynchotrema

Insect:  Mosquito, Wood tick and Corn borer

Mascot:  Gopher (*Citellus tridecemlineatus*)

Mineral:  Iron ore

Parasite:  Leech and legislator

Slogan:  No sales tax and Come fall in love with a loon

Soil:  Lester loam

Reptile:  Blanding's turtle

# HISTORY

In 1635 the region was first explored by French fur traders.

Region claimed for France by Daniel Greysolon, sieur de Duluth in 1679.

The region east of the Mississippi was ceded by France to England in 1763. England ceded this region to the United States in 1783. The remaining future state of Minnesota was acquired by the United States from France as part of the Louisiana Purchase in 1803.

In 1819 Fort St. Anthony was established as the first settlement. Fort St. Anthony was renamed Fort Snelling in 1824.

Minnesota Territory was created in 1849.

During the Civil War Chief Little Crow of the Sioux Indian tribe led a bloody uprising in which over 500 white settlers were killed. The Sioux were defeated at Wood Lake in 1862 and driven from the state.

Mesabi Range iron ore deposits were discovered in 1890.

The Better Business Bureau was founded at Minneapolis in 1912.

In 1944 the Farmer Labor party merged with the Democratic party.

# FACTS AND TRIVIA

Mayo Clinic in Rochester is world renowned for state of the art methods of treatments. Branches of the Mayo Clinic are in Florida and Arizona.

The largest regional theater in the country is the Guthrie Theater.

In 1849 Henry Sibley chose the motto for the territorial seal *Quae sursum volo videre or* "I wish to see what is above". It was engraved *Quo sursum velo videre or* "I cover to see what is above". *L'etoile du Nord* was adopted in 1861 as motto for the state seal.

The biggest mansion in the midwest is James J. Hill House in St. Paul. The house was constructed in 1891.

Mall of America is the largest shopping complex in the nation.

Lumbertown U. S. A. has 30 buildings and a general store. The town is a replica of an 1870 lumber town.

The skyway system connects 52 blocks of downtown Minneapolis.

Minnesota has over 10,000 lakes.

The largest urban sculpture garden in the country is in Minneapolis.

Fort Snelling over looks the Mississippi River. The restored stone fort is located in St. Paul.

The state capital building in St. Paul has the largest free standing marble dome in the world. It was constructed in 1905.

Chanhassen Dinner Theater in Minneapolis is the largest dinner theater in the country.

Duluth on Lake Superior is the largest U. S. inland port.

The first bone marrow transplant and the first open heart surgery were done at the University of Minnesota.

Bemidji is home to giant statues of Paul Bunyan and Babe the Blue Ox.

The American Swedish Institute is located in Minneapolis. Minnesota has the largest population of Scandinavians in the United States.

# MISSISSIPPI

Mississippi:  Mississippi comes from the Ojibwa Indian word *misi sipi* which means great river.

Capital:  Jackson

Flower:  Magnolia (*Magnolia grandiflora*) 1952

Tree:  Magnolia (*Magnolia grandiflora*) 1938

Bird:  Mockingbird (*Mimus polyglottos*) 1944

Waterfowl:  Wood duck (*Aix sponsa*) 1974

Nickname:  The Magnolia State

Rank:  20 (December 10, 1817)

Motto:  *Virtute et Armis* (By valor and arms)

Song:  Go, Mississippi by Houston Davis 1962

Stone:  Petrified wood 1976

Shell:  Oyster shell (*Crassostrea virginica*) 1974

Fossil:  Prehistoric whale (*Zygorhiza kochii*), Eocene 1981

Land Mammal:  White tailed deer (*Odocoileus virginianus*) 1974

Insect:  Honeybee (*Apis mellifera*) 1980

Butterfly:  Spicebush swallowtail butterfly (*Pterorus troilus*) 1991

Water Mammal:  Bottle-nosed dolphin or porpoise (*Tursiops truncatus*) 1974

Fish:  Largemouth bass (*Micropterus salmoides*) 1974

Beverage:  Milk 1984

Coat of Arms:  Mississippi Coat of Arms 1894

# HISTORY

In 1540 Spanish explorer Hernando de Soto made an expedition to Mississippi. He discovered the Mississippi River in 1541.

The Mississippi Valley was claimed for France by Rene Robert Cavelier de La Salle in 1682.

Fort Maurepas was built on Biloxi Bay by Pierre Le Moyne, sieur d'Iberville in 1699.

Fort Rosalie in Natchez was established in 1716.

In 1763 the region was ceded by the French to the British. The British ceded their claim to the United States after the War of Independence. Spain ceded their claim to the region in the Treaty of San Lorenzo in 1795. The boundaries of Mississippi were extended after the Louisiana Purchase.

The region was organized into Mississippi Territory in 1798.

Natchez became the first capital of Mississippi in 1817.

In 1861 Jefferson Davis became president of the Confederacy.

Vicksburg, a major port on the Mississippi River was seized in 1863. After the Civil War, plantation owners in Mississippi were bankrupted by the freeing of slaves. Union troops left widespread destruction in Mississippi.

Petroleum was discovered in 1939.

James H. Meredith became the first black enrolled in the University of Mississippi in 1962.

In 1963 civil rights leader Medgar Evers was assassinated in Jackson.

White civil rights workers Andrew Goodman, Michael Schwener and James Cheney were killed in 1964.

# FACTS AND TRIVIA

The largest river in the United States is the Mississippi River. It is the chief waterway in the nation and is nicknamed "Old Man River".

Lumberton is home to the largest pecan nursery in the world.

On January 8, 1935 Elvis Presley "The King of Rock and Roll" was born in Tupelo, Mississippi.

The poorest state in the nation is Mississippi.

Ingalls Division of Litton Industries in Pascagoula builds most of the complex ships for the United States Navy.

The Order of the Eastern Star originated in Mississippi.

Memorial Day was the result of a kind gesture in Friendship Cemetery on April 25, 1866. The graves of both Union and Confederate soldiers were decorated with flowers by the ladies of Columbus.

Petal is home to the International Checkers Hall of Fame.

The second largest national cemetery in the country is the Vicksburg National Cemetery.

Beauvoir was the last home of Jefferson Davis and is preserved in Biloxi.

The first lung transplant in the world was performed at the University of Mississippi Medical Center in 1963. In 1964 the first heart transplant surgery in the world was accomplished by Dr. James D. Hardy.

# MISSOURI

Missouri: The name Missouri is from the Iliniwek Indian word *missouri* meaning owner of big canoes.

Capital: Jefferson City

Floral Emblem: White hawthorn blossom of the red haw or wild haw (*Crateagus*) 1923

Tree: Flowering dogwood (*Cornus florida*) 1955

Bird: Bluebird (*Sialia sialis*) 1927

Nickname: The Show Me State

Rank: 24 (August 10, 1821)

Motto: *Salus Populi Suprema Lex Esto* (The welfare of the people shall be the supreme law)

Song: Missouri Waltz by J. R. Shannon, John V. Eppel and Frederic Knight Logan 1949

Musical Instrument: Fiddle 1987

Folk Dance: Square dance 1995

Rock: Mozarkite 1967

Mineral: Lead ore (*Galena*) 1967

Fossil: Crinoid or crinoidea (*Delocrinus missouriensis*), Carboniferous 1989

Animal: Missouri mule  A mule is the sterile hybrid offspring of a male donkey and a female horse.  1995

Insect: Honeybee (*Apis mellifera*) 1985

Aquatic Animal: Paddlefish or spoonbill (*Polyodon spathula*) 1997

Fish: Channel catfish (*Ictalurus punctatus*) 1997

Nut: Eastern black walnut (*Juglans nigra*) 1990

Day: Missouri Day or the third Wednesday in October 1915

# HISTORY

Hernando de Soto explored the area in 1541.

France claimed the region based on explorations by Jacques Marquette, Louis Jolliet and Rene Robert Cavelier de La Salle in 1682.

The first settlement was made at Ste. Genevieve by lead miners and French hunters in 1735.

In 1763 Spain controlled the region but ceded it to France in 1800.

St. Louis was settled by Pierre Laclade in 1765.

France sold the region as part of the Louisiana Purchase in 1803.

The 1811-1812 New Madrid earthquakes were 8.6 on the Richter scale.

In 1860 the Pony Express from St. Joseph to Sacramento began.

During the Civil War in 1861 the state was divided over the slavery issue but the majority remained loyal to the Union.

At St. Joseph, Jesse James was killed by a fellow gang member in 1882.

Bagnell Dam was completed on the Missouri River in 1931.

Winston Churchill gave the iron curtain speech at Fulton in 1952.

In 1965 the 630 foot stainless steel Gateway Arch designed by architect Eero Saarinen was completed in St. Louis. The arch commemorates the American westward migration.

## FACTS AND TRIVIA

St. Louis is nicknamed Home of the Blues and the Gateway to the West.

In Kansas City, Missouri the Harry S. Truman Library and Museum exhibits Truman memorabilia.

Jefferson City was designated state capital in 1826. The first two capital buildings burned. The present third capital building was occupied in 1918.

The Pony Express National Memorial is in St. Joseph.

Missouri is the premier mule producer of the nation. A mule is the offspring of a female horse and a male donkey. Missouri mules pulled pioneer wagons, aided farmers and moved troops and supplies during WWI and WWII.

The headquarters of Hallmark Cards is in Kansas City.

In Kansas City the site of the first daylight robbery by the James gang was restored and is called the Jesse James Bank Historic Site.

Mark Twains Boyhood Home and Museum are in Hannibal.

The original site of the city of St. Louis was restored into a business and entertainment center. This nine square block area is called Lacledes Landing.

Art collections featuring Federic Remington and Thomas Hart Benton are exhibited at the Nelson Atkins Museum of Art in Kansas City.

Six Flags Over Mid-America theme park is in St. Louis.

Daniel Boone was active in the development of the state of Missouri. He moved from Kentucky to Missouri in 1795.

Missouri Day was adopted by the state primarily due to the efforts of Mrs. Anna Brosius Korn. It honors the state, its people and all their achievements.

Adophus Busch the brewer was a native of Missouri. The Anheuser Busch Brewery in St. Louis offers tours demonstrating brewing techniques.

# MONTANA

Montana:  In Spanish the word *montana* means mountainous.
Capital:  Helena
Flower:  Bitterroot (*Lewisia rediviva*) 1895
Tree:  Ponderosa pine (*Pinus ponderosa*) 1949
Bird:  Western meadowlark (*Sturnella neglecta*) 1931
Nickname:  The Treasure State, The Mountain State, Big Sky Country,
           Bonanza State or Land of Shining Mountains
Rank:  41 (November 8, 1889)
Motto:  *Oro y Plata* (Gold and silver)
Song:  Montana by Charles C. Cohan and Joseph E. Howard 1935
Ballad Song:  Montana Melody by LeGrande and Carleen Harvey 1983
Gemstones:  Montana sapphire and agate 1969
Fossil:  Maiasaura or duck billed dinosaur (*Maiasaura peeblesorum*),
         Cretaceous 1985
Animal:  Grizzly bear (*Ursus arctos horribilis*) 1983
Fish:  Black spotted cutthroat trout (*Oncorhynchus clarki*) 1977
Grass:  Bluebunch wheat grass (*Agropyron spicatum pursh*) 1973
Metal:  Metal of Valor 1985
Memorial Garden:  Veterans Memorial Rose Garden in Missoula,
                  Montana 1999
Vietnam Veterans Memorial:  Rose Park in Butte, Montana 1987
Korean Veterans Memorial:  Stoddard Park in Butte, Montana 1997

# HISTORY

In 1740 French trappers and explorers came to the area.

French explorer Sieur de la Verendrye explored the region in 1742.

The United States acquired most of Montana from France in the Louisiana Purchase and the rest of the state was part of the original Oregon country.

Meriwether Lewis and William Clark explored the region in 1805.

The first fur fort was built by Manuel Lisa on the Yellowstone River in 1807. Fort Union an American fur company post was constructed in 1828 at the mouth of the Yellowstone River.

In 1841 missions were established among the Flathead Indians. St. Marys was established by Father Pierre Jean de Smer in the Bitterroot Valley.

The first permanent settlement of the region was in 1846 at Fort Benton.

In 1862 gold was discovered in Grasshopper Creek located in southwestern Montana. Mining camps quickly grew around the gold fields. The two biggest gold camps were Bannack and Virginia City.

The region was organized and it became the Montana Territory in 1864.

On June 25, 1876 Lieutenant Colonel George Armstrong Custer and five troops of Calvary were slain by Sioux Indians under Sitting Bull at the Battle of the Little Bighorn.

Marcus Daly established the town of Anaconda and its smelting works after he discovered copper near Butte in 1880.

In 1909 homesteaders entered the state of Montana.

The Fort Peck Dam was completed in 1940.

In 1983 Anaconda Copper mining operations were closed in Butte.

Over 3,000 disciples of the Church Universal and Triumphant awaited nuclear cataclysm in under ground shelters at Paradise Valley under the direction of Elizabeth Prophet in 1990.

## FACTS AND TRIVIA

Little Bighorn Battlefield National Monument is just south of Billings.

Sapphires from Montana are the only gemstones from North America included in the Crown Jewels of England. These sapphires were thrown away by miners during the gold rush because they clogged up mining screens.

Montana is the only place Tyrannosaurus Rex fossils have been found.

Dinosaur eggs were found at Egg Mountain near Choteau that were more like birds and mammals than like reptiles.

There are seven Indian reservations in Montana.

Glacier National Park is the most visited place in Montana. The park is adjacent to Waterton Lakes National Park in Canada. The combined parks form the Waterton-Glacier International Peace Park.

Cooked bitterroot supplemented the diets of early Indian tribes.

Giant Springs is the largest freshwater spring in the United States. Roe River flows near Great Falls from this spring. This river is one of the smallest rivers in the world. The length of the river varies from 58 feet to 200 feet.

The World Museum of Mining and Copper King Mansion are in Butte.

# NEBRASKA

Nebraska: Nebraska is from the Oto word *nebrathka* which means flat water.

Capital: Lincoln

Flower: Goldenrod (*Soldiago gigantea*) 1895

Tree: Cottonwood (*Populus deltoides marsh*) 1972

Arbor Day Centennial Tree: Green Ash (*Fraximus pennsylvanica*) 1972

Bird: Western meadowlark (*Sturnella neglecta*) 1929

Nickname: The Cornhusker State 1945 The state was formerly called The Tree Planters State and The Great American Desert.

Rank: 37 (March 1, 1867)

Motto: Equality before the law

Song: Beautiful Nebraska by Jim Fras 1967

Ballad Song: A Place Like Nebraska by Sol Kutler 1997

Folk Dance: Square dance 1997

Gemstone: Chalcedony or blue agate 1967

Rock: Prairie agate 1967

Fossil: Woolly mammoth (*Mammuthus*), Pleistocene *Archidiskodon imperator maibeni* mammoth found in Lincoln County is reported to be the largest elephant in the world. 1967

Soil: Holdrege series 1979

Grass: Little bluestem (*Andropogon scoparius or schizachyrium scoparium scoparium*) 1969

Mammal: White tailed deer (*Odocoileus virginianus*) 1981

Insect: Honeybee (*Apis mellifera*) 1975

Fish: Channel catfish (*Ictalurus punctatus*) 1997

Beverage: Milk 1998

Soft Drink: Kool-aid Developed in Hastings by Edwin E. Perkins in 1927. 1998

Historic Baseball Capital: St. Paul, Nebraska 1997

Baseball Capital: Wakefield, Nebraska 1997

Village of Lights: Cody, Nebraska 1997

River: Platte River 1998

State Poet Laureate: John G. Neihardt (1881-1973) 1921

State Poet: William Kloefkorn 1982

Arbor Day: Founded by J. Sterling Morton of Nebraska City in 1872.

# HISTORY

Francisco Vasquez de Coronado explored the region in 1541.

In 1763 France ceded the region to Spain. Spain returned the land to France in 1800.

The United States purchased the land from Napoleon as part of the Louisiana Purchase in 1803.

Meriwether Lewis and William Clark crossed the region in 1804.

Bellevue near Omaha was the first permanent settlement in 1823.

The region was set aside as Indian Territory in 1834.

In 1854 Nebraska became a separate territory. It was created by the Kansas-Nebraska Bill which divided Missouri Territory into Nebraska Territory and Kansas Territory.

The 1862 free land terms of the Homestead Act caused many Civil War veterans to settle in Nebraska.

To encourage tree planting Nebraska became the first state to observe Arbor Day in 1872. Nebraska City is the site of Arbor Lodge State Park. The park was created to honor J. Sterling Morton the founder of Arbor Day.

Ranchers went bankrupt when thousands of cattle died in the severe winter of 1886-1887.

The dust bowl in the 1930's caused many people to leave Nebraska.

Unicameral or single house legislature was adopted in 1937. Nebraska is the only state with a unicameral legislature.

In 1939 oil was discovered in Nebraska.

# FACTS AND TRIVIA

The largest Mammoth elephant fossil in the world was found in Lincoln County. Archidiskodon imperator maibeni is on display at the University of Nebraska State Museum in Lincoln.

Fort Robinson State Park is located in Crawford. It is an old frontier military post which was established in 1874 and the site of Chief Crazy Horse's death.

In 1895 Nebraska was first nicknamed "The Tree Planters State" because of the states pioneer efforts in tree planting and for the founding of Arbor Day.

There is an abundance of agate in the Ogallala National Grasslands.

Buffalo Bill Ranch State Historical Park is in North Platte. The home of Buffalo Bill Cody and memorabilia of his Wild West Show are at the park.

The Ogallala aquifer in Nebraska is the largest underground lake water supply in the United States.

Boys Town is a self contained community of homeless and underprivileged boys which was founded by Rev. Edward J. Flanagan west of Omaha.

The American Elm (*Ulmus americana l.*) was adopted as Nebraska's state tree in 1937. Since so many of the elm trees in Nebraska were killed by Dutch Elm disease the state decided to adopt the cottonwood as state tree in 1972.

"Cornhuskers" was coined in 1900 by Charles S. Sherman who was a sportswriter for the Nebraska State Journal in Lincoln.

# NEVADA

Nevada:  The Spanish word *nevada* means snow covered sierra.
Capital:  Carson City
Flower:  Sagebrush (*Artemisia tridentata*) 1917 and 1967
Trees:  Single leaf pinon or pinon pine (*Pinus monophylla*) 1959
         Bristlecone pine (*Pinus aristata*) 1987
Bird:  Mountain bluebird (*Sialia currucoides*) 1967
Nickname:  The Sagebrush State, The Battle Born State or The Silver
         State
Rank:  36 (October 31, 1864)
Motto:  All for our country
Song:  Home Means Nevada by Mrs. Bertha Raffetto 1933
Gemstone:  Virgin Valley black fire opal 1987
Semiprecious Gemstone:  Nevada turquoise 1987
Rock:  Sandstone 1987
Metal:  Silver (*Ag*) 1977
Fossil:  Ichthyosaur, extinct marine reptile or fish lizard (*Shonisaurus*
        *popularis*), Triassic 1977
Animal:  Desert bighorn sheep (*Ovis canadensis nelsoni*) 1973
Reptile:  Desert tortoise (*Gopherus agassizii*) 1989
Fish:  Lahontan cutthroat trout (*Onchorhynchus clarki henshawi*) 1981
Grass:  Indian rye grass (*Oryzopsis hymenoides*) 1977
Artifact:  Tule duck decoy 1995
Colors:  Silver and blue 1983
Slogan:  "Battle Born"  This refers to Nevada becoming a state
        during the Civil War.  1937

# HISTORY

The area was first explored by Spanish explorer Francisco Tomas Garces in 1775.

In 1843 an exploring party led by John C. Fremont visited the area.

The United States acquired the region at the end of the Mexican War in 1848 with the Mexican cession.

In 1849 the first settlement in Nevada was founded as Mormon Station. This settlement is now called Genoa.

Nevada was made a part of Utah Territory in 1850.

The state of Nevada developed rapidly when silver was discovered in the Comstock Lode region in 1859. Gold was discovered later southeast of the Comstock region.

Nevada became a separate territory in 1861.

In 1931 gambling was legalized in Nevada.

The Hoover Dam was built in 1935.

In 1951 nuclear tests were conducted at Yucca Flats.

# FACTS AND TRIVIA

The Liberty Bell was a slot machine invented by Charles Fey in 1899. This machine is the prototype for all slot machines. In 1999 there was one slot machine for every ten people or 205,726 slot machines in Nevada.

Guinness World of Records Museum is in Las Vegas. Many of the world's biggest and best are on display at the museum.

Kangaroo rats in Death Valley can live without drinking liquid.

There are more hotel rooms in Las Vegas than in any other place in the world. Most of the largest hotels in the world are in Las Vegas.

The Thunderbirds Aerobatic Demonstration Team is at Nellis Air Force Base in Las Vegas.

Hoover Dam contains 3.25 million cubic yards of concrete. Lake Mead is formed by 726 foot high Hoover Dam and has 822 miles of shoreline.

Houdini Theater in Las Vegas features live magic acts and is part of The Magic and Movie Hall of Fames over 500 exhibits.

Adolph Hitler's 1939 Mercedes Benz is one of the many automobiles on display at the Imperial Palace Auto Collection in Las Vegas.

The Nevada Gambling Museum is located in Virginia City. The historic mining town of Virginia City is called the liveliest ghost town in the west.

Pair-O-Dice Club was the first casino to open on the future Las Vegas Strip in 1931. Big name entertainment, theme parks, luxury hotels and 24 hour gambling casinos are located on the world famous Las Vegas Strip.

A prehistoric Pueblo village called the Lost City is now under Lake Mead. Pueblo Indian artifacts are displayed at Lost City Museum in Overton.

The Liberace Museum is in Las Vegas. A large collection of his gemstone capes, trademark candelabras, and expensive cars are on display.

Most of Nevada is desert and it receives less rainfall than any other state.

The gambling industry generates half of the tax revenues for Nevada.

# NEW HAMPSHIRE

New Hampshire: The state is named for the English county of
Hampshire.

Capital: Concord

Flower: Purple lilac (*Syringa vulgaris*) 1919

Wildflower: Pink lady slipper (*Cypripedium acaule*) 1991

Tree: White birch (*Betula papyrifera*) 1947

Bird: Purple finch (*Carpodacus purpureus*) 1957

Nickname: The Granite State

Rank: 9 (June 21, 1788)

Motto: Live free or die

Songs: Old New Hampshire by Dr. John F. Holmes and Maurice
Hoffmann 1949

New Hampshire, My New Hampshire by Julius Richelson and
Walter P. Smith 1963

New Hampshire Hills by Paul Scott Mowrer and Tom Powers
1963

Autumn In New Hampshire by Leo Austin 1977

New Hampshire's Granite State by Anne B. Currier 1977

Oh, New Hampshire (You're My Home) by Brownie McIntosh
1977

The Old Man Of The Mountain by Paul Belanger 1977

The New Hampshire State March by Rene Richards 1977

New Hampshire Naturally by Rick Shaw and Ron Shaw 1983

Gemstone: Smoky quartz

Mineral: Beryl  A gemstone which is commonly found in granite rocks.
1985

Rock: Granite 1985

Animal: White tailed deer (*Odocoileus virginianus*) 1983

Insect: Ladybug (*Coccinellidae*) 1977

Butterfly: Karner blue or Melissa blue butterfly (*Lycaeides melissa
samuelis*), endangered 1992

Amphibian: Spotted newt (*Notophthalmus viridescens*) 1985

Freshwater Fish: Brook trout (*Salvelinus fontinalis*) 1994

Saltwater Game Fish: Striped bass (*Roccus saxatilis*) 1994

Sport: Skiing 1998

# HISTORY

In 1603 English explorer Martin Pring visited the coastal area.

John Smith explored the coast in 1614.

Under an English land grant Captain John Mason in 1623 sent David Thomson and Edward and Thomas Hilton to establish two fishing colonies. Thomson settled at Little Harbor later called Rye and the Hilton brothers settled at Northam which was renamed Dover.

From 1679-1698 the region was a royal province under John Cutt.

The region was under the jurisdiction of Massachusetts from 1698-1741.

New Hampshire was again made a royal province from 1741-1766.

Indian raids were stopped by Rogers Rangers in 1759.

The citizens of Portsmouth were warned of a potential British troop landing on April 18, 1775 by Paul Revere which resulted in the British fort being raided by patriots. Munitions from the raid were used at the Battle of Bunker Hill. The royal governor Sir John Wentworth fled to Nova Scotia.

In 1803 the first textile mill was built.

Sino-Russian War was ended by the Treaty of Portsmouth in 1905. New Hampshire is the only state to host the formal conclusion of a foreign war.

The International Monetary Fund was established in 1944.

In 1963 New Hampshire became the first state to support public education by adopting a lottery.

# FACTS AND TRIVIA

In 1719 the first potato was planted in the United States. The potato was planted at Londonderry Common Field.

Peterborough was the site of the first American public library in 1833.

There are more than 40 historic buildings in Portsmouth. Historic Strawberry Banke is one of the oldest neighborhoods in America.

New Hampshire has been called the "Mother of Rivers". Five of the major rivers of New England originate in New Hampshire. The Connecticut, Merrimack, Piscataqua, Saco and Salmon Falls rivers all originate in the state.

The aerial tramway in Franconia Notch was the first in the United States to be erected to a mountain top.

Kancamagus Highway is a 34 mile scenic route between Conway and North Woodstock through White Mountain National Forest.

Mount Washington's summit is 6,288 feet. It is the highest mountain north of the Mason Dixon Line and east of the Rockies.

The first cog railroad to Mount Washington dates to 1869.

In 1952 the first U. S. Presidential Primary was held in New Hampshire.

There are 40,000 miles of rivers and streams and 1,300 lakes or ponds in New Hampshire. Bodies of water cover over 115,000 acres of New Hampshire.

Skiing is enjoyed into July and August in New Hampshire. Cranmore skimobile, Tuckerman, Cannon, Sunapee and Gilford slopes are popular lifts.

New Hampshire's constitution is the second oldest in the country. The constitution was adopted in 1784.

# NEW JERSEY

New Jersey: The state was named for the English Channel Island of Jersey.

Capital: Trenton

Flower: Common meadow violet (*Viola sororia*) 1971

Tree: Red oak (*Quercus borealis maxima*) 1950

Memorial Tree: Dogwood (*Cornus*) 1951

Bird: American goldfinch (*Carduelis tristis*) 1935

Nickname: The Garden State or The Diner Capital of the World

Rank: 3 (December 18, 1787)

Motto: Liberty and prosperity

Song: I'm From New Jersey by Red Mascara (Unofficial)* The song passed both houses in 1972.

Folk Dance: Square dance 1983

Dinosaur: Hadrosaur or duck billed herbivorous reptile (*Hadrosaurus foulkii*), Cretaceous 1991

Shell: Knobbed whelk or conch shell (*Busycon carica gmelin*) 1995

Animal: Horse (*Equus caballus*) 1977

Insect: Honeybee (*Apis mellifera*) 1974

Fish: Brook trout (*Salvelinus fontinalis*) 1991

Colors: Buff and jersey blue  General George Washington chose these colors for New Jersey troops during the War of Independence.

Tall Ship: *A. J. Meerwald* 1998

# HISTORY

The region was explored by Giovanni de Verrazano in 1524.

In 1609 Henry Hudson explored the Hudson River.

A Dutch trading post was built in 1618 at Bergen on the Hudson River.

Fort Nassau was established by Dutch settlers in 1623.

In 1664 the region was taken from the Dutch by the English. The Duke of York granted the land to Sir George Carteret and Lord John Berkeley.

During the War of Independence, New Jersey was a major battleground. The Continental Army fought over one hundred battles in the state.

In 1800 women were given the right to vote in Elizabethtown.

Voting rights were restricted to men in 1807.

In 1934 the passenger ship Morro Castle burned killing 134 people.

The Hindenburg exploded while docked at Lakehurst in 1937.

In 1952 the New Jersey Turnpike opened.

There were race riots at Newark in 1967 which left 26 dead.

Gambling was legalized in Atlantic City in 1978.

The strictest gun legislation in the United States was adopted by the state of New Jersey in 1990.

## FACTS AND TRIVIA

The most densely populated state in the United States is New Jersey. All of the counties in New Jersey are classified as metropolitan areas.

Hoboken was the site where the first baseball game was played.

More cars are stolen in Newark then in any other city. North Jersey is called the "Car Theft Capital of the World".

Headquarters for the Boy Scouts of America is in New Brunswick.

New Jersey is known as the "Diner Capital of the World". There are more diners in the state than in any other place in the world.

The Statue of Liberty and Ellis Island are in New Jersey.

New Jersey is the largest chemical producing state in the nation.

In 1858 the first nearly intact and complete dinosaur skeleton was discovered. The Hadrosaurus foulkii skeleton was also the first dinosaur to be displayed for public view. It was discovered in Haddonfield by William Foulke. Hadrosaurus foulkii was a 25 foot eight ton duck billed plant eating reptile.

New Jersey grows two thirds of the worlds supply of eggplant.

The first boardwalk in the world was in Atlantic City.

Morristown National Historical Park is where George Washington was headquartered from 1779-1780.

Camden was the site of the first drive-in movie theater.

The largest seaport in the United States is located in Elizabeth.

Thomas Edison invented the light bulb, motion picture projector and record player in his New Jersey laboratory. His office, laboratories and work-shops are located west of Newark at the Edison National Historic Site.

Atlantic City is host to the annual Miss America Pageant.

The tallest water tower in the world is in New Jersey.

# NEW MEXICO

New Mexico: The state was named by Spanish explorers after Mexico.
Capital: Santa Fe
Flower: Yucca flower (*Yucca glauca*) 1927
Tree: Pinon pine or pine nut (*Pinus edulis*) 1948
Bird: Roadrunner or chaparral bird (*Geococcyx californianus*) 1949
Nickname: Land of Enchantment
Rank: 47 (January 6, 1912)
Motto: *Crescit Eundo* (It grows as it goes) 1882
Song: O' Fair New Mexico by Elizabeth Garrett 1917
Spanish Language Song: Asi Es Nuevo Mexico by Amadeo Lucero 1971
Ballad: The Land Of Enchantment New Mexico by Michael Martin
        Murphy, Chick Raines and Don Cook 1989
Bilingual Song: New Mexico (*Mi Lindo Nuevo Mexico*) 1995
Gemstone: Turquoise 1967
Fossil: Coelophysis or small carnivorous dinosaur, Triassic 1981
Animal: Black bear (*Ursus americanus*) 1975
Insect: Tarantula hawk wasp (*Pepsis formosa*) 1989
Fish: New Mexico or Rio Grande cutthroat trout (*Oncorhynchus clarki
        virginalis*) 1955
Grass: Blue grama grass (*Bouteloua gracillis*) 1973
Cookie: Bizcochito 1989
Vegetables: Chili pepper (*Capsicum annum*) 1965
            Frijol or pinto bean (*Phaseolus vulgaris*) 1965
Dish: Chili
Colors: Red and yellow  These were the colors of old Spain.  1925
Balloon Museum: Anderson-Abruzzo International Balloon Museum
                1999
Poem: *A Nuevo Mexico* by Luis Tafoya 1991
Slogan: Everybody is Somebody in New Mexico 1975
Question: Red or green?  This jokingly refers to the chili peppers which
        are popular to residents.

# HISTORY

Ancient cliff dwellers and their descendants the Pueblo Indians were the first inhabitants of the region.

In 1539 Franciscan Marcos de Niza visited the region in search of gold.

The principle explorers of the region were Cabeza de Vaca, Francisco Vasquez de Coronado and Nuno de Guzman.

From 1588 -1599 Juan de Onate conquered the region. He founded the first settlement at San Gabriel.

Santa Fe was founded in 1605 and became the states capital in 1710.

Early settlers traded and fought with the Navajo, Apache and Comanche. In 1680 there was a great Indian revolt which expelled all of the Spanish from the region until it was reconquered by the Spanish in 1692.

The area became a province of the Republic of Mexico in 1821.

In 1846 Mexican-American War was declared.

The land was ceded to the United States after the Mexican-American War ended in 1848 under the terms of the Treaty of Guadalupe Hidalgo.

From 1850-1863 the region was organized into a territory.

Cattlemen staged the Lincoln County War against merchants from 1878 - 1881. The outlaw William "Billy the Kid" Bonney played a leading role.

In 1942 Los Alamos was selected as the first research and development facility for nuclear weapons.

Alamagordo Air Base was where the first atom bomb was exploded on July 16, 1945.

# FACTS AND TRIVIA

One of the oldest public buildings in America is the Palace of Governors in Santa Fe. It was built in 1810.

Chaco Culture National Historical Park is believed to be the center of the Chaco Anasazi civilization.

The "Uranium Capital of the World" is Grants.

At the annual "Whole Enchilada Fiesta" in Las Cruces the largest enchilada in the world is made the first weekend in October.

Acoma Pueblo is thought to be the oldest continuously inhabited site in the United States. Many of the ancient ruined cities are in New Mexico.

The "Green Chile Capital of the World" is Hatch.

Fort Sumner is where William "Billy the Kid" Bonney is buried.

At 7,000 feet Santa Fe is the highest capital city in the United States.

Fort Union National Monument is the site of the largest military post in the southwest. Fort Union guarded the Santa Fe Trail from 1850-1890.

Carlsbad Caverns National Park has some of the largest limestone caverns and the largest natural cave room in the world.

Kit Carson's home and the Indian community of Taos Pueblo are in Taos.

There is a higher percentage of Native Americans living in New Mexico than in any other state.

The largest gypsum deposit is at White Sands National Monument.

# NEW YORK

New York:  The state was named in honor of the Duke of York or James II of England.

Capital:  Albany

Flower:  Any rose cultivated or wild (*Rosa*) 1955

Tree:  Sugar maple (*Acer saccharum*) 1956

Bird:  Bluebird (*Sialia sialis*) 1970

Nickname:  The Empire State or The Big Apple

Rank:  11 (July 26, 1788)

Motto:  *Excelsior* (Ever upward)

Song:  I Love New York by Steve Karmen

Gem:  Wine red garnet 1969

Fossil:  Sea scorpion (*Eurypterus remipes*), Silurian 1984

Shell:  Bay scallop (*Argopecten irradians*) 1988

Animal:  Beaver (*Castor canadensis*) 1975

Insect:  Ladybug or 9 spotted ladybird beetle (*Coccinella novemnotata*) 1989

Fish:  Brook trout (*Salvelinus fontinalis*) 1975

Beverage:  Milk 1981

Fruit:  Apple (*Malus*) 1976

Muffin:  Apple muffin 1987

Slogan:  I Love New York 1977

# HISTORY

In 1524 Giovanni de Verrazano discovered New York harbor and part of the Hudson River.

The St. Lawrence River was explored in 1603 by Samuel de Champlain.

In 1609 the Hudson River was explored by Henry Hudson.

The region was claimed by the Dutch and called New Netherland.

Fort Orange was established by the Dutch in 1614.

The colony of New Amsterdam was founded in 1625 by Peter Minuit on Manhattan Island.

In 1664 New Amsterdam was seized by the British and renamed New York. The British also changed the name of Fort Orange to Albany.

Benjamin Franklin proposed a plan for the federal union of the colonies in 1754. His plan was the forerunner of the Declaration of Independence.

The British fleet took control of New York City in 1776.

In 1782 General George Washington established headquarters for the Continental Army at Newburgh. During the Revolutionary War ninety two of the over three hundred battles were fought in New York.

In 1789 George Washington was inaugurated president in New York City.

West Point was founded in 1802 by the United States Military Academy.

The Statue of Liberty was dedicated in 1886.

In 1901 President William McKinley was assassinated in Buffalo.

New York City is where UN headquarters was established in 1945.

In 1959 the St. Lawrence Seaway opened.

# FACTS AND TRIVIA

The tallest building in New York is the 110 story World Trade Center.

MTA New York City transit subway has the most stations with 486.

The home of George Eastman the founder of Eastman Kodak is now the International Museum of Photography in Rochester.

Niagara Reservation was the first state park in the United States.

Niagara Falls is actually three falls: Bridal Veil Falls and American Falls in America and Horseshoe Falls in Canada.

The Franklin D. Roosevelt National Historic Site is in Hyde Park.

Alexander Hamilton established "The New York Post" in 1803. It is the oldest running newspaper in the United States.

The 1980 Winter Olympics was held at Lake Placid.

Taughannock is the highest waterfall in New York.

Union College in Schenectady is called the "Mother of Fraternities". Delta Phi, Sigma Phi and Kappa Alpha were started at Union College.

The National Baseball Hall of Fame and Museum is in Cooperstown.

Legends of Rip Van Winkle were born in the Catskills.

A meatpacker from Troy named Sam Wilson is where "Uncle Sam" originated. Soldiers during the War of 1812 saw U. S. Beef stamped on his products and interpreted that as Uncle Sam.

The first railroad in America was between Albany and Schenectady.

# NORTH CAROLINA

North Carolina:  In 1629 King Charles I of England created this
province.  Carolina was derived from *carolus* which
is Latin for Charles.

Capital:  Raleigh

Flower:  Dogwood (*Cornus*) 1941

Tree:  Pine (*Pinus*) 1963

Bird:  Cardinal (*Cardinalis cardinalis*) 1943

Nickname:  The Tar Heel State or The Old North State

Rank:  12 (November 21, 1789)

Motto:  *Esse Quam Videri* (To be rather than to seem) 1893

Song:  The Old North State by William Gaston and Mrs. E. E. Randolph
1927

Precious Stone:  Emerald 1973

Rock:  Granite 1979

Shell:  Scotch bonnet (*Phalium granulatum*) 1965

Mammal:  Grey squirrel (*Sciurus carolinensis*) 1969

Dog:  Plott hound (*Canis lupis familiaris*) 1989

Insect:  Honeybee (*Apis mellifera*) 1973

Reptile:  Eastern box turtle (*Terrapene carolina carolina*) 1979

Saltwater Fish:  Channel bass or red drum (*Sciaenops ocellata*) 1971

Beverage:  Milk 1987

Vegetable:  Sweet potato 1995

Historical Boat:  Shad boat 1987

Colors:  Red and blue 1945

Toast:  The Tar Heel Toast 1957

# HISTORY

In 1585 the English attempted to colonize the region but returned to England.

Sir Walter Raleigh established another colony in 1587 on Roanoke Island. The colonists disappeared without a trace and became known as the "Lost Colony". Virginia Dare was born on August 18, 1587. She was the first child of English parents born in the New World.

King Charles II granted Carolina to eight proprietors in 1663.

In 1677 the colonists rebelled to unfair tax collection policies. It was called Culpeppers Rebellion.

North and South Carolina were separated in 1710.

The proprietors sold their rights back to the Crown in 1729.

In 1775 the royal governor was driven out by the colonists.

The first province to vote for independence was North Carolina in 1776.

North Carolina in 1829 established the first state university system in the United States.

In 1838 the Cherokees were driven out of North Carolina into Oklahoma.

North Carolina was the last state to secede from the Union on May 20, 1861. It was readmitted in 1868.

The American Tobacco Company was founded in 1890.

Kitty Hawk, North Carolina was the site of the first successful airplane launch by the Wright brothers in 1903.

In 1979 twelve Ku Klux Klansmen were charged with first degree murder after a confrontation with demonstrators which resulted in five deaths.

# FACTS AND TRIVIA

The oldest state university in the United States is the University of North Carolina Chapel Hill.

One of the largest homes in America is the Biltmore Estate in Asheville.

Fort Raleigh National Historic Site is the site of Sir Walter Raleigh's "Lost Colony".

The "Furniture Capital of the World" is High Point.

World War II battleship *USS North Carolina* was saved from scrap by public donations in the 1960's and is moored as a memorial in Wilmington.

At Reed Gold Mine Historic Site near Concord you can pan for gold.

Calvary Church is the largest church complex in the nation. The complex is home to the largest pipe organ in the southeast.

The 480 foot Fontana is the tallest dam in the eastern United States.

Krispy Kreme Doughnut originated in Winston-Salem.

Whitewater Falls is the highest waterfall in the eastern United States.

The first U. S. mint built outside of Washington is now The Mint Museum of Art in Charlotte.

Cherry Point in Havelock is the largest air base in the Marine Corps.

Charlotte Observer Omnimax Theater has the most advanced projector ever built.

# NORTH DAKOTA

North Dakota:  The Sioux Indian word *dakota* means friends or allies.
Capital:  Bismarck
Flower:  Wild prairie rose (*Rosa blanda or arkansana*) 1907
Tree:  American elm (*Ulmus americana*) 1947
Bird:  Western meadowlark (*Sturnella neglecta*) 1947
Nickname:  The Peace Garden State 1957  The state is also called The
        Sioux State, The Flickertail State and The Roughrider State.
Rank:  39 (November 2, 1889)
Motto:  Liberty and union, now and forever, one and inseparable
Creed:  North Dakota Creed by Frank L. McVey (Unofficial) 1926
Song:  North Dakota Hymn by James W. Foley and Dr. C. S. Putnam
March:  Flickertail March (Spirit Of The Land) by James D. Ployhar
        1975
Dance:  Square dance 1995
Fossil:  Teredo petrified wood, Paleocene  The teredo was a worm
        shaped mollusk related to oysters, clams and mussels which
        burrowed into trees.  1967
Grass:  Western wheat grass (*Agropyron smithii*) 1977
Honorary Equine:  Nokota horse (*Equus caballus*) 1993
Fish:  Northern pike (*Esox lucius*) 1969
Beverage:  Milk 1983
Language:  English 1987
Coat of Arms:  North Dakota Coat of Arms 1957

# HISTORY

The area was claimed for France in 1682 by Rene Robert La Salle.

In 1762 France transferred their claim of the region to Spain.

Part of the region was obtained by the British in 1763.

The United States in the Louisiana Purchase of 1803 received the land which was not claimed by the British.

Meriwether Lewis and William Clark explored the area from 1804-1806.

The first settlement was at Pembina in 1812 by Scots-Canadians.

In 1818 the remainder of the region was obtained by the United States from the British.

Fort Union was built by the American Fur Company at the mouth of the Yellowstone River in 1829.

Steamboats from the Missouri River reached the territory in 1838.

The first military outpost Fort Abercrombie was established in 1857.

Dakota was organized into a territory in 1861.

In 1863 homesteading was opened in the Dakota Territory.

Dakota Territory was divided into North and South Territories in 1889.

North Dakota was the first state to hold a presidential primary in 1912.

Lake Sakakawea was formed when the Garrison Dam was completed.

North Dakota legalized gambling in 1981.

In 1997 agriculture was devastated by the Red River floods.

## FACTS AND TRIVIA

Minot Air Force Base located outside Minot has personnel from all over the world. Their motto is "Only the best come north".

Fort Union National Historical Site commemorates the Fort Union Trading Post. From 1829-1867 this trading post was the principal fur trading depot in the upper Missouri River region.

The annual Turtle Racing Championship is held at Turtle Lake. At the entrance of Turtle Lake there is a two ton sculpture of a turtle.

In Bismarck at the entrance to the North Dakota Heritage Center there is a twelve foot bronze statue of Sakakawea with her baby strapped to her back.

The International Peace Garden is on the international boundary between Canada and North Dakota. Peace between the United States and Canada is commemorated by the formal gardens and colorful flower beds.

In 1883 President Theodore Roosevelt established the Maltese Cross Ranch and the Elkhorn Ranch. They are included in the Theodore Roosevelt National Park which is a scenic region along the Little Missouri River called the Badlands.

Jamestown is the site of the largest buffalo monument in the world.

Sioux leader Sitting Bull was killed in 1890 when an attempt was made to arrest him during the Ghost Dance unrest. His original grave is commemorated by the Sitting Bull Burial State Historic Site at Fort Yates.

Fort Lincoln State Park near Bismarck marks the start of Custer's ride to the Little Big Horn in Wyoming where he and 655 of his men were killed.

# OHIO

Ohio:  Ohio is derived from the Iroquois word *oheo* which means beautiful.

Capital:  Columbus 1816

Flower:  Red or scarlet carnation (*Dianthus caryophyllus*)  In memory of President William McKinley who always wore a red carnation. 1904

Wildflower:  Large white trillium (*Trillium grandiflorum*) 1987

Tree:  Ohio Buckeye (*Aesculus globra*) 1953

Bird:  Cardinal (*Cardinalis cardinalis*) 1933

Nickname:  The Buckeye State

Rank:  17 (March 1, 1803)

Motto:  With God, all things are possible 1958

Song:  Beautiful Ohio by Ballard MacDonald, Wilbert B. McBride and Mary Earl 1969

Rock Song:  Hang On Sloopy by Rick Derringer  It was first recorded by the McCoys. 1985

Gemstone:  Flint  Early settlers and native Americans used flint to make knifes, millstones, flintlock guns, spear points and arrowheads. 1965

Fossil:  Isotelus, trilobite or extinct sea creature similar to a horseshoe crab, Ordovician 1985

Animal:  White tailed deer (*Odocoileus virginianus*) 1988

Insect:  Ladybug or ladybird beetle (*Coccinellidae*) 1975

Reptile:  Black racer snake (*Coluber constrictor*)  It is called the farmers friend because this snake eats disease carrying rodents.  1995

Fish:  Walleye (*Stizostedion vitreum vitreum*), Unofficial*

Beverage:  Tomato juice 1965

# HISTORY

Prehistoric Indians called Mound Builders were the first recorded inhabitants of the region. These Indians belonged to the Hopewell culture.

In 1669 Rene Robert Cavelier de La Salle visited the area.

Moravian missionaries founded a settlement they called Schoenbrunn in 1772. The settlement of Schoenbrunn was destroyed in 1776.

The region was controlled by the British from 1763-1783.

After the Revolutionary War the land was ceded to the United States.

The first permanent settlement of the region was founded by General Ruffus Putnam at Marietta in 1788. Marietta was named in honor of French Queen Marie Antoinette.

General "Mad" Anthony Wayne defeated the Tecumseh Indians in 1794 at the battle of Fallen Timbers. The Greenville Treaty was signed in 1795.

In 1811 William H. Harrison beat the Tecumseh Indians at the battle of Tippecanoe.

The British fleet was defeated by Oliver Hazard Perry at the battle of Put-in-Bay in 1813.

In 1832 the Ohio and Erie Canals were completed.

The Dayton flood in 1913 killed 400 people in the Miami River Valley and there was an estimated 100 million dollars in damages.

Carl B. Stokes was the first black mayor of a major city in the United States. He was elected mayor of Cleveland in 1967.

In 1970 the National Guard killed four students who were protesting the Vietnam War at Kent State University.

# FACTS AND TRIVIA

Burial mounds of the Hopewell Indians are preserved at Mound City National Monument in Chillicothe.

Some of the largest accessible glacial grooves in the world are on the north side of Kelleys Island.

The Rock and Roll Hall of Fame and Museum is in Cleveland.

Cleveland restored Shoenbrunn the first settlement in Ohio.

In 1924 long jumper DeHart Hubbard of Ohio became the first African-American to win an Olympic gold medal.

The first traffic light was constructed on August 5, 1914 in Cleveland.

In 1810 Chillicothe became the first capital of Ohio.

Astronaut Neil Armstrong became the first man to walk on the moon on July 20, 1969. He was a native of Wapakoneta.

The first professional baseball team was the Cincinnati Reds.

New Concord native John Glenn was the first American to orbit the earth in 1962. In 1998 he became the oldest American to travel into space.

Chewing gum was patented in 1869 by W. F. Semple of Mount Vernon.

In 1839 Charles Goodyear developed vulcanized rubber in Akron. The "Rubber Capital of the World" is Akron, Ohio.

The Pro Football Hall of Fame is in Canton.

# OKLAHOMA

Oklahoma: Oklahoma is from the Choctaw Indian word *okla humma* which means land of the red people.

Capital: Oklahoma City

Floral Emblem: Mistletoe (*Phoradendron serotinum*) 1893

Wildflower: Indian blanket (*Gaillardia pulchella*)

Tree: Redbud (*Cercis canadensis*) 1937

Bird: Scissor tailed flycatcher (*Muscivora forficata*) 1951

Game Bird: Wild turkey (*Meleagris gallopavo*)

Nickname: The Sooner State "Sooners" were settlers who entered to claim land before the official start of a land rush.

Rank: 46 (November 16, 1907)

Motto: *Labor Omnia Vincit* (Labor conquers all things)

Song: Oklahoma by Oscar Hammerstein II and Richard Rodgers 1953

Waltz: Oklahoma Wind

Country Western Song: Faded Love

Children's Song: Oklahoma, My Native Land by Martha Kemm Barrett

Musical Instrument: Fiddle

Percussive Musical Instrument: Drum

Folk Dance: Square dance

Rock: Barite rose rock 1968

Soil: Port silt loam

Animal: American buffalo (*Bison americanus*) 1972

Furbearer Animal: Raccoon (*Procyon loter*)

Game Animal: White tailed deer (*Odocoileus virginianus*)

Insect: Honeybee (*Apis mellifera*) 1992

Butterfly: Black swallowtail butterfly (*Papilio polyxenes*) 1996

Reptile: Mountain boomer or collared lizard (*Crotophytus collaris*) 1969

Fish: White or sand bass (*Morone chrysops*) 1974

Colors: Green and white 1915

Salute: Oklahoma flag salute "I salute the flag of the state of Oklahoma. Its symbols of peace unite all people".

Poem: *Howdy Folks* by David Randolph Milsten 1973

Grass: Indian grass (*Sorghastrum nutans*) 1972

Beverage: Milk

Theater: Lynn Riggs Players of Oklahoma, Inc.

Monument: The Golden Driller (Larry) in Tulsa, Oklahoma

Pin: OK pin

# HISTORY

In 1541 Francisco Vasquez de Coronado explored the area.

The region was part of the Louisiana Purchase in 1803.

In 1830 the Indian Removal Act deported Indians from the southeast. Some of the land in Oklahoma was set aside for these Indians.

Cherokee, Choctaw, Chickasaw, Creek and Seminole Indians left the southeast and traveled to Oklahoma on "The Trail of Tears" (1828-1846). Comanche, Osage and other Plains Indians also occupied the region.

The territory was opened to homesteaders by runs and lottery in 1889. Fifty thousand people participated in the first run on April 22, 1889. The Cherokee Outlet in 1893 was the most famous run.

Oklahoma Territory was organized in 1890.

Bartlesville commercial oil well was completed in 1897.

The Indians wanted Indian Territory to be independent of Oklahoma Territory and attempted to become a separate state in 1905.

In 1907 President Theodore Roosevelt merged Oklahoma Territory and Indian Territory. Oklahoma became a state on November 16, 1907.

To stop violence Governor John C. Walton declared martial law in 1923. The governor was impeached.

The Federal building in Oklahoma City was bombed by Timothy McVeigh in 1995. There were 168 people killed in the explosion.

# FACTS AND TRIVIA

In 1889 Oklahoma was opened by land rush. Early settlers were allowed to claim land by grabbing stakes which marked the plots during land rushes. "Sooners" entered to claim the land before the land rush officially started.

There is a working oil derrick on the grounds of the states capital.

The National Cowboy Hall of Fame is in Oklahoma City.

Anadarko is host to the annual American Indian Exposition. The Indian Hall of Fame is also in Anadarko.

The part of Oklahoma which borders Red River is called "Little Dixie".

Natives of Oklahoma are called "Okies".

Alabaster and onyx like formations are at Alabaster Caverns State Park in one of the largest gypsum caves in the world.

Humorist Will Rogers Memorial is in Claremore.

There is a dinosaur quarry at Black Mesa State Park in northwestern Oklahoma near Boise City.

Oklahoma Territorial Museum is in Guthrie.

The states first commercial oil well was Nellie Johnstone in Bartlesville.

Robbers Cave State Park east of McAlester is were Jesse James and his gang retreated to hideout.

The Seminole Nation Museum is in Shawnee.

Native Americans give craft demonstrations in a recreated village at the Cherokee Heritage Center in Tahlequah. Tahlequah has been the capital of the Cherokee Nation since 1839.

# OREGON

Oregon:  Originally the state was called *Ouragan* which is French for hurricane.

Capital:  Salem

Flower:  Oregon grape (*Mahonia aquifolium*) 1899

Tree:  Douglas fir (*Pseudotsuga menziesii*) 1939

Bird:  Western meadowlark (*Sturnella neglecta*) 1927

Nickname:  The Beaver State

Rank:  33 (February 14, 1859)

Motto:  *Alis Volat Proiis* (She flies with her own wings)  The motto is attributed to Judge Jessie Quinn Thornton.  1987

Song:  Oregon, My Oregon by J. A. Buchanan and Henry B. Murtagh 1927

Dance:  Square dance 1977

Gemstone:  Oregon sunstone (*Feldspar*) 1987

Rock:  Thunderegg geode 1965

Seashell:  Oregon hairy triton (*Fusitriton oregonensis*) 1991

Animal:  Beaver (*Castor canadensis*) 1969

Insect:  Oregon swallowtail butterfly (*Papilio oregonius*) 1979

Fish:  Chinook, spring, king or tyee salmon (*Oncorhynchus tshawytscha*) 1961

Beverage:  Milk 1997

Nut:  Hazelnut (*Corylus avellana*) 1989

Father of Oregon:  Dr. John McLoughlin 1957

Mother of Oregon:  Tabitha Moffatt Brown 1987

Team:  Oregon Trail Blazers

# HISTORY

In 1543 Spanish explorers from Mexico explored the coast.

British explorer Sir Francis Drake visited the region in 1578.

Captain James Cook explored area for Great Britain in 1778.

In 1792 George Vancouver explored the area.

Captain Robert Grey explored the mouth of Columbia River. He claimed the region for the United States in 1792.

In 1805 Meriwether Lewis and William Clark explored the mouth of the Columbia River.

Astoria was established in 1811 by the Pacific Fur Company.

Claims to the region were relinquished to the United States by: Spain (1819), Russia (1825) and Britain (1846).

Settlements were made in the Willamette River Valley in 1829.

The Oregon Trail was traveled by many settlers in 1843 and a provisional government was established.

Oregon was organized as a territory in 1848.

The railroad was completed in 1883.

In 1937 the Bonneville Dam was completed.

Oregon was declared a disaster area in 1964 due to severe rain and snow. There were 40 deaths as a result of the storm.

The "bottle law" was first enacted by Oregon in 1972.

In 1975 navigation to Astoria, Oregon from Lewiston, Idaho became possible on the Snake River.

## FACTS AND TRIVIA

The 8,000 foot deep Hells Canyon in northeastern Oregon is the deepest river gorge in North America.

Ulric Ellerhusens statue "Oregon Pioneer" tops the state capitol building.

Oregon was the first state to require statewide voter registration.

Ninety nine percent of the commercial Hazelnut crop in the United States is grown in Oregon. Dorris Ranch in Springfield was Oregon's first orchard.

"Old Perpetua" a geyser in Lakeview blows water 60 feet into the air.

The deepest lake in the United States is Crater Lake in Klamath County. An ancient volcano formed the depression which is now Crater Lake.

Sea Lion Caves was discovered near Florence in 1880. It is the largest sea cave in the world and is home to several hundred sea lions.

Portland is called the "City of Roses".

Mount Hood a dormant volcano is the tallest peak in Oregon.

The only national scenic area in the United States is the Columbia Gorge National Scenic Area east of Portland.

Oregon is the leading grower of Christmas trees in the United States.

The site of an early Willamette River settlement is at Champoeg State Park outside Newberg.

Malheur, Wasco, Jefferson, Wheeler and Crook counties are where the state rock of Oregon the thunderegg is found.

# PENNSYLVANIA

Pennsylvania:  The state was named for the father of William Penn founder of Pennsylvania commonwealth.

Capital:  Harrisburg

Flower:  Mountain laurel (*Kalmia latifolia*) 1933

Tree:  Eastern hemlock (*Tsunga canadensis*) 1931

Game Bird:  Ruffed grouse (*Bonasa umbellus*) 1931

Nickname:  The Keystone State

Rank:  2 (December 12, 1787)

Motto:  Virtue, liberty and independence

Song:  Pennsylvania by Eddie Khoury and Ronnie Bonner 1990

Fossil:  Trilobite (*Phacops rana*), Devonian 1988

Animal:  White tailed deer (*Odocoileus virginanus*) 1959

Dog:  Great dane (*Canis lupis familiaris*) 1965

Insect:  Firefly (*Poturis pennsylvanica de geer*) 1974 and 1988

Fish:  Brook trout (*Salvelinius fontinalis*) 1970

Beverage:  Milk 1982

Flagship:  United States brig *Niagara* 1988

Plant:  Penngift crown vetch (*Coronilla varia l. penngift*) The plant was chosen for beautification and conservation.  1982

Coat of Arms:  Pennsylvania Coat of Arms 1875

# HISTORY

Cornelis Jacobssen explored Delaware Bay in 1614.

The first settlers were Swedish. Tinicum Island was the site of the first settlement in 1643. It was seized by the Dutch in 1655. The British took control of the settlement in 1664.

William Penn an English Quaker was granted a proprietary charter by King Charles II in 1681. King Charles II wanted to get rid of the Quakers.

The southern boundary of Pennsylvania was established from 1763-1767. This boundary is known as the Mason Dixon Line. The boundary later became the line between slave and no slave states.

In 1776 the Declaration of Independence was signed in Philadelphia.

During the Revolutionary War George Washington and the Continental Army made winter quarters at Valley Forge in 1777. Valley Forge National Historic Park commemorates the site of Washington's headquarters.

In Philadelphia the Constitution was signed in 1787. Pennsylvania was the second state to ratify the Constitution.

The turning point of the Civil War was the Battle of Gettysburg in 1863. The Gettysburg Address was given by Lincoln in 1863. Gettysburg National Military Park commemorates this great Civil War battle.

The Johnstown flood of 1889 was the worst flood in United States history. There were 2,200 people killed in the disaster.

In 1892 at Homestead Steel Works in Pittsburgh 12 strikers were killed.

There were 20 coal miners killed in 1897 during a strike.

In Philadelphia there was a three day race riot in 1964. Over 500 people were injured in the riot.

The Three Mile Island nuclear reactor had a partial melt down in 1979.

Water supplies in Pennsylvania, Ohio and West Virginia were disrupted in 1988 when over 713,000 gallons of diesel fuel spilled into the Monongahela River from a storage tank.

# FACTS AND TRIVIA

Independence National Historical Park in Philadelphia preserves history from 1774-1800 in Christ Church, Congress Hall, Franklin Court, Graff House, Independence Hall, Liberty Bell Pavilion and Old City Hall.

The "Chocolate Capital of the United States" is Hershey.

In 1859 Titusville became the site of the first oil well in the world.

Philadelphia was where the first Continental Congress convened in 1774. It was the capital of the United States from 1790-1800.

Pennsylvania was the first state to abolish slavery in 1780.

Philadelphia is known as "The City of Brotherly Love".

The first bank was chartered in Pennsylvania. It was chartered in 1781 and called the Bank of North America.

Betsy Ross made the first American flag in Philadelphia.

Punxsutawney is called "Weather Capital of the World" because of its weather forecasting groundhog Punxsutawney Phil.

# RHODE ISLAND

Rhode Island: Rhode Island was named for the Mediterranean island of Rhodes.

Capital: Providence

Flower: Violet (*Viola palmata*) 1968

Tree: Red maple (*Acer rubrum*) 1964

Bird: Rhode Island red chicken (*Gallus*) 1954

Nickname: Little Rhody or The Ocean State

Rank: 13 (May 29, 1790)

Motto: Hope

Song: Rhode Island It's For Me by Charlie Hall, Maria Day and Kathryn Chester 1946

Mineral: Bowenite  This mineral is a close relative of Jade. 1966

Shell: Quahog or quahaug (*Mercenaria mercenaria*)  The quahog is a thick shelled edible clam. 1987

Rock: Cumberlandite  This is a magnetic rock which is found on both sides of Narragansett Bay but not found north of Cumberland. 1966

Fish: Brook trout (*Salvelinus fontinalis*), Unofficial*

Coat of Arms: Rhode Island Coat of Arms

# HISTORY

In 1636 religious exile Roger Williams was expelled from Massachusetts because of his religious beliefs. He purchased land near the present Providence from Indians in the Narragansett Bay region. Newport was founded in 1639.

Rhode Island was a principal refuge for those persecuted due to their religious beliefs during the colonial period. In 1657 the colony gave protection to Quakers. The colony also gave protection to Jews from Holland in 1658.

In King Philips War from 1675-1676 colonists defeated the Narragansett Indians in what was called the Great Swamp Fight.

The British revenue cruiser Gaspee was burned by colonists in 1772. The colonists were angered by British trade restrictions.

Rhode Island became the first colony to renounce allegiance to Britain. The colony declared its independence on May 4, 1776.

On May 29, 1790 Rhode Island became the last colony to ratify the Constitution. It was fearful of the larger states taking control of the smaller states. Rhode Island was forced to ratify the Constitution by threats of cutting off trade and annexation.

Newport was the site of the first Americas Cup Race in 1930.

In 1969 the Newport Bridge was completed across Narragansett Bay.

The Americas Cup Race in 1983 was won by the first non-United States boat in 132 years. The boat was named the Australia II.

# FACTS AND TRIVIA

In 1638 Roger Williams founded the first Baptist church in North America at Providence. Roger Williams is acknowledged as the originator of the concepts reflected in the First Amendment which are the freedoms of religion, speech and assembly.

Rhode Island and Providence Plantations is the official name of the state.

Newport was the site of the first Quaker meeting house in 1699.

In the foyer of the State House there is a reproduction of the original Liberty Bell. The United States Treasury Department gave the bell to the people of Rhode Island in 1950.

Rhode Island was the site of the first open golf tournament in 1985.

Cumberlandite the official state rock of Rhode Island is found on both sides of Narragansett Bay. The rock will attract a magnet.

The Touro Synagogue in Newport is the oldest synagogue in the U. S.

Rhode Island is the smallest state in the United States.

Jacqueline Bouvier and John Fitzgerald Kennedy were married in 1953 at St. Marys church in Rhode Island.

The Tennis Hall of Fame is in Newport.

In Adamsville the Rhode Island Red Monument honors the poultry breed.

The Independent Man is an 11 foot bronze statue which was placed on top of the State House on December 18, 1899.

In Providence the Capital contains a full length portrait of George Washington. The portrait was done by portraitist Gilbert Stuart of Wickford.

# SOUTH CAROLINA

South Carolina:  The state was named for King Charles II.  Carolina is derived from the word *carolus* which is Latin for Charles.

Capital:  Columbia

Flower:  Carolina yellow jessamine (*Gelsemium sempervirens*) 1924

Tree:  Cabbage palmetto or Inodes palmetto (*Sabal palmetto*) 1939

Bird:  Carolina wren (*Thryothorus lucovicianus*) 1948

Game Bird:  Wild turkey (*Meleagris gallopavo*) 1976

Nickname:  The Palmetto State or The Iodine State

Rank:  8 (May 23, 1788)

Motto:  *Dum Spiro Spero* (While I breathe, I hope)

Songs:  Carolina (Patriotic) by Henry Timrod and Anne Custis Burgess 1911

South Carolina On My Mind by Hank Martin and Buzz Arledge 1984

Music:  The spiritual 1999

Folk Dance:  Square dance 1994

Dance:  The shag 1984

Gemstone:  Amethyst 1969

Stone:  Blue granite 1969

Shell:  Lettered olive (*Oliva sayana*) 1984

Animal:  White tailed deer (*Odocoileus virginianus*) 1972

Dog:  Boykin spaniel (*Canis lupis familiaris*) 1985

Insect:  Carolina mantis or praying mantis (*Stagmomantis carolina johannson*) 1988

Butterfly:  Eastern tiger swallowtail butterfly (*Pterourus glaucus*) 1994

Reptile:  Loggerhead sea turtle (*Caretta caretta*) 1988

Amphibian:  Spotted salamander (*Ambystoma maculatum*) 1999

Fish:  Striped bass (*Morone saxatilis*) 1972

Beverage:  Milk 1984

Hospitality Beverage:  Tea (*Camellia sinensis*) 1995

Fruit:  Peach 1984

Botanical Garden:  Clemson University Botanical Garden 1992

Poet Laureate:  Bennie Lee Sinclair (Mrs. Don Lewis) 1934

# HISTORY

The region was visited by Spanish explorers in 1520.

England claimed the region based on John and Sebastian Cabots voyage.

The land was granted to Sir Robert Heath in 1629 by King Charles I. No attempts were made by Sir Robert Heath to establish settlements.

In 1663 eight proprietors were given grant to the land by King Charles II. A colony was established and named Carolina.

Charlestown was the first settlement in 1670. The settlement was moved and renamed Charles Town and in 1783 Charles Town was named Charleston.

Carolina was divided into North Carolina and South Carolina in 1729.

During the Revolutionary War Francis Marion was a leader in many battles. Francis Marion became known as the "Swamp Fox". He confused the British with guerrilla combat tactics rather than engaging the British in their traditional British combat.

South Carolina was the first state to secede from the Union in 1860.

The opening shots of the Civil War were on April 12, 1861 with the bombardment of Fort Sumter in Charleston Harbor.

General Sherman's Army made its famous "March to the Sea". There was tremendous damage to the state especially along Sherman's route. During the reconstruction period South Carolina was one of the worst sufferers.

Both Savannah, Georgia and Charleston, South Carolina experienced a cyclone which resulted in 1,000 deaths in 1893.

The Savannah River nuclear plant begin production in 1951 at Aiken. The plant was closed in 1988 for safety reasons.

In 1989 24 people were killed and over 6 billion dollars in property damage done by hurricane Hugo.

# FACTS AND TRIVIA

The premier resort of Myrtle Beach is in the center of the Grand Strand which is a 60 mile section of beach on the coast of South Carolina.

Congaree Swamp National Monument is near Columbia.

South Carolina is one of the leading peach producers in the nation. The "Peach Capital of the World" is Johnston.

Edisto River is the longest flowing blackwater stream in the world.

There is an elevated water storage tank shaped like a peach in Gaffney.

Brookgreen Gardens near Myrtle Beach displays over 500 sculptures by American artists in their picturesque gardens.

South Carolina is the only state to have produced tea commercially.

Established in 1773 the Charleston Museum is the oldest in the nation.

The Pendleton District Agricultural Museum displays the first boll weevil found in South Carolina.

There have been sightings of a Loch Ness type monster in Lake Murray.

Upper Whitewater Falls is the highest cascade in eastern America.

The oldest minor league stadium in the nation is Duncan Park Baseball Stadium in Spartanburg.

# SOUTH DAKOTA

South Dakota:  The Sioux Indian word *dakota* means friends or allies.
Capital:  Pierre
Flower:  Pasque flower, may day flower or prairie crocus (*Pulsatilla hirsutissima*) 1903 and 1919
Tree:  Black Hills white spruce (*Picea glauca densata*) 1947
Bird:  Chinese ring necked pheasant (*Phasianus culchicus*) 1943
Nickname:  The Coyote State, The Sunshine State or The Mount Rushmore State
Rank:  40 (November 2, 1889)
Motto:  Under God, the people rule
Song:  Hail! South Dakota (March) by Deecort Hammitt 1943
Gemstone:  Fairburn agate 1966
Jewelry:  Black Hills gold or tricolor gold designed in grapes and leaves 1988
Mineral:  Rose quartz 1966
Fossil:  Triceratops or horned dinosaur, Cretaceous 1988
Grass:  Western wheat grass (*Agropyron smithii*) 1970
Animal:  Coyote (*Canis latrans*) 1949
Insect:  Honeybee (*Apis mellifera*) 1978
Fish:  Walleye (*Stizostedion vitreum vitreum*) 1982
Greeting:  *How, Kola!*  This is Indian for hello friend.
Slogan:  "Great Faces, Great Places"  The slogan refers to the famous faces of Mount Rushmore and all the other interesting people and places in South Dakota.

# HISTORY

French Canadian explorers Les Verendrye and his brother visited the region in 1743. They buried a lead plate to prove they had claimed the region for France. The plate that was buried in 1743 was not found until 1913.

The United States acquired the land in the Louisiana Purchase of 1803.

In 1804 and 1806 Meriwether Lewis and William Clark passed through the area.

Fort Pierre was the first white American settlement in 1817. The fort was a trading post in 1831 and became a military post in 1855.

Sioux Falls was founded in 1857.

The region was organized as part of the Dakota Territory in 1861.

Dakota Territory was reduced to its current boundaries in 1863.

Gold was discovered in the Black Hills in 1874. Miners rushed into the Sioux Indian Reservation. The U. S. tried but failed to stop the miners.

Custer was defeated by the Sioux at the Little Big Horn in 1876.

In 1877 Sioux Indians relinquished the land. This gave rise to the great Dakota Boom in 1879.

North and South Dakota were divided and attained statehood in 1889.

Sioux Indians and their families were massacred at the Battle of Wounded Knee in 1890.

In 1892 there was a great land rush when nine million acres of former Sioux Indian lands were sold.

The courthouse at Wounded Knee was taken over by AIM or the American Indian Movement for ten weeks in 1973.

# FACTS AND TRIVIA

Washington, Jefferson, Lincoln and Theodore Roosevelt are sculpted on the granite face of Mount Rushmore in the Black Hills. The busts by Gutzon Borgium are proportionate to men 465 feet tall.

The geographic center of the United States is near Belle Fourche.

Rapid City is called the gateway to the Black Hills. Mount Rushmore National Memorial, Crazy Horse Memorial, Jewel Cave National Monument, Wind Cave National Park and Badlands National Park are all located near Rapid City.

The largest petrified wood park in the world is in Lemmon.

Homestake Mine in Lead is the largest underground gold mine in the world. The mine was the largest gold producer in the Western Hemisphere.

Yankton was the capital of Dakota when it was a territory.

The state capitol building in Pierre which was originally completed in 1910 is one of the most fully restored state capitols in the United States.

Black Hills gold jewelry is exclusively designed and manufactured in the Black Hills of South Dakota.

The grave of James Butler better known as "Wild Bill Hickok" is in the famous gold rush town of Deadwood in Mount Moriah Cemetery. Jack McCall the man who murdered "Wild Bill Hickok" was hung in Yankton.

# TENNESSEE

Tennessee: The state of Tennessee was named after a village of the Cherokees called *Tenase* or it was derived from the Yuchi Indian word *Tana* which means the meeting place.

Capital: Nashville

Cultivated Flower: Purple iris or any iris (*Iridaceae*) The most common purple iris is blue flag. 1933 and 1973

Wildflower: Passion flower (*Passiflora*) or maypop (*Passiflora incarnata*) 1973

Tree: Tulip poplar (*Liriodendron tulipifera*) 1947

Bicentennial Tree: Yellowwood (*Cladastis lutea*) 1991

Bird: Mockingbird (*Mimus polyglottos*) 1933

Game Bird: Bobwhite quail (*Colinus virginianus*) 1988

Nickname: The Volunteer State 1812

Rank: 16 (June 1, 1796)

Motto: Agriculture and commerce

Songs: My Homeland Tennessee by Neil Grayson Taylor and Roy Lamont Smith 1925

When It's Iris Time In Tennessee by Willa Wald Newman 1935

My Tennessee (public school) by Frances Hannah Tranum 1955

Tennessee Waltz by Redd Stewart and Pee Wee King 1965

Rocky Top by Boudleaux and Felice Bryant 1982

The Pride Of Tennessee by Fred Congdon, Thomas Vaughn and Carol Elliot 1996

Tennessee by Vivian Rorie 1992

Folk Dance: Square dance 1980

Gem: Tennessee river pearls They are uncultured pearls made by mussels in fresh water rivers. 1979

Rocks: Agate 1969

Limestone (*Calcium carbonate*) 1979

Wild Animal: Raccoon (*Procyon lotor*) 1972

Insects: Firefly (*Photinus pyralls*) 1975

Ladybug (*Coccinellida*) 1975

Agricultural Insect: Honeybee (*Apis mellifera*) 1990

Butterfly: Zebra swallowtail butterfly (*Eurytides marcellus*) 1995

Reptile: Eastern box turtle (*Terrapene carolina*) 1995

Amphibian: Tennessee cave salamander (*Gyrinophilus palleucus*) 1995

Commercial Fish: Channel catfish (*Ictalurus punctatus*) 1988

Game Fish: Largemouth bass (*Micropterus salmoides*) 1988

Bicentennial Poem: *Who Are We* by Margaret Britton Vaughn 1996

Poem: *Oh Tennessee, My Tennessee* by Admiral William Lawrence 1973

Poet Laureate: Margaret Britton Vaughn 1999

Slogan: Tennessee, America at its Best 1965

# HISTORY

Spanish explorer Hernando de Soto explored the Memphis area in 1541.

In 1663 the region was claimed by England as part of the Carolina grant.

Fort Prudhomme was built in 1682 by French explorer La Salle.

French settlers established Fort Assumption in 1714 near Nashville.

Fort Loudoun near Knoxville was established by English settlers in 1756.

In 1763 after the French and Indian War France gave up its claim.

Colonists from Virginia and North Carolina established permanent settlements in the valleys of the Holston and Watauga Rivers in 1769.

Daniel Boone and other pioneers founded the state of Transylvania and created a settlement at Nashville in 1780 but the new state was not sanctioned.

The region was organized as Territory South of the Ohio in 1790.

Cherokee Indians in Tennessee were moved to Oklahoma in the 1830's.

In 1843 Nashville was chosen as the permanent capital of Tennessee.

Tennessee and Virginia were the main battlegrounds for the Civil War. Famous battles fought during the Civil War in Tennessee include: Shiloh (1862), Chattanooga (1863), Stones River (1863) and Nashville (1864).

The state seceded from the Union in 1861 and was readmitted in 1866.

In 1925 Clarence Darrow defended John T. Scopes who was convicted of violating the ban on teaching evolution in public schools.

The Tennessee Valley Authority was created in 1933.

Oak Ridge was the site of the first operational nuclear reactor in 1943.

At the Lorraine Motel in Memphis, Tennessee Martin Luther King was assassinated in 1968. The motel is now the National Civil Rights Museum.

# FACTS AND TRIVIA

Tennessee has had four towns to serve as its state capital. Knoxville, Kingston, Murfreesboro and Nashville have all been designated as its capital.

Graceland in Memphis was the home of Elvis Presley. It is the second most visited house in the country.

Ruby Falls and Rock City Gardens are in Chattanooga.

Nashville is home to the Country Music Hall of Fame and Museum and Opryland U. S. A. which includes the Grand Old Opry.

The states capitol building was constructed of marble quarried in Tennessee. It was designed by architect William Strickland who died during the construction from 1845-1859 and had himself buried within its walls.

Symbolized by the Parthenon, Nashville is called Athens of the South.

Reelfoot Lake in Union County was formed in 1812 during the New Madrid Earthquake. It was the largest earthquake in American history.

The Hermitage in Nashville was home of 7th president Andrew Jackson.

Great Smoky Mountains National Park is the most visited national park in the United States. It is noted for the blue haze which envelopes its forests.

There is a large underground lake in Sweetwater called the "Lost Sea".

Tennessee was nicknamed "The Volunteer State" when more soldiers volunteered to fight in the war with Mexico than had been requested.

# TEXAS

Texas: The name Texas comes from the Hasinal Indian word *Tejas* meaning friends or allies.

Capital: Austin

Flower: Bluebonnet, buffalo clover, wolf flower or el conejo (*Lupinus subcarnosus*) 1901 and any other variety of bluebonnet 1971

Tree: Pecan (*Carya illinoensis*) 1919

Bird: Mockingbird (*Mimus polyglottos*) 1927

Nickname: The Lone Star State

Rank: 28 (December 29, 1845)

Motto: Friendship 1930

Song: Texas, Our Texas by William J. Marsh and Gladys Yoakum Wright 1929

Flower Song: Bluebonnets by Julia D. Booth and Lora C. Crockett 1933

Musical Instrument: Guitar 1997

Folk Dance: Square dance 1991

Gem: Texas blue topaz 1969

Gemstone Cut: The lone star cut 1977

Stone: Petrified palmwood (*Palmoxylon*), Oligocene 1969

Shell: Lightning whelk (*Busycon perversum pulleyi*) 1987

Dinosaur: Brachiosaur sauropod (*Pleurocoelus*), Cretaceous 1997

Small Mammal: Armadillo (*Dasypus novemcinctus*) 1995

Large Mammal: Texas longhorn cow (*Bos bos*) 1995

Flying Mammal: Mexican free tailed bat (*Brasilia tadarida*) 1995

Insect: Monarch butterfly (*Danaus plexippus*) 1995

Reptile: Horned lizard (*Phrynosoma cornutum*) 1993

Fish: Guadalupe bass (*Micropterus treculi*) 1989

Grass: Sideoats grama (*Bouteloua curtipendula*) 1971

Fruit: Texas red grapefruit (*Citrus paradisi*) 1993

Vegetable: Sweet onion (*Allium*) 1997

Native Pepper: Chiltepin (*Capsicum annuum*) 1997

Pepper: Jalapeno (*Capsicum annuum*) 1995

Plant: Prickly pear cactus (*Opuntia*) 1995

Dish: Chili 1977

Fiber and Fabric: Cotton 1997

Ship: *USS Texas* 1995

Sport: Rodeo 1997

Plays: *The Lone Star, Texas, Beyond the Sundown, and Fandangle* 1979

Bluebonnet City: Ennis, Texas 1997

Bluebonnet Festival: Chappell Hill Bluebonnet Festival 1997

Bluebonnet Trail: Ennis, Texas 1997

Air Force: Confederate Air Force 1989

Tartan: Texas bluebonnet 1991

# HISTORY

The Gulf coast was mapped in 1519 by Alonso Alvarez de Pineda.

Ysleta near El Paso was the site of the first Spanish settlement in 1682.

In 1685 Rene Robert Cavelier de La Salle attempted to claim the region for France by founding a colony on Matagorda Bay.

The region was occupied by Spain in 1715.

In the Louisiana Purchase of 1803 the United States acquired the claim France had made for the region.

The United States relinquished their claim of the region to Spain in 1819.

Mexico won independence from Spain in 1821. Texas was then made a province of Mexico.

Texas declared its independence from Mexico in 1836 and became the Republic of Texas. Mexican General Santa Anna was victorious at the Battle of the Alamo leaving no survivors. Davy Crockett, Jim Bowie and William Travis were among the 189 brave Texans who died defending the Alamo against 2,500 Mexican soldiers. Sam Houston subsequently annihilated the Mexican Army at San Jacinto. The victory at San Jacinto ended Mexican sovereignty over Texas.

Texas seceded from the Union in 1861 and was readmitted in 1870.

The worst natural disaster in United States history occurred in Galveston when 6,000 people were killed by a hurricane and tidal wave in 1900.

Oil was discovered in 1901.

Houston became the site of the NASA Space Center in 1962.

In 1963 President John F. Kennedy was assassinated in Dallas, Texas.

# FACTS AND TRIVIA

There is a 570 foot monument at the San Jacinto Battleground State Park near Houston which commemorates the 1836 Battle of San Jacinto.

The most popular historic site in Texas is the Alamo in San Antonio.

Six Flags Astroworld is a 75 acre theme park in Houston.

Famous Texan Sam Houston was actually born in Virginia and served as governor of Tennessee before coming to Texas. Sam Houston Memorial Museum is in Huntsville and Sam Houston Park is in Houston.

On July 20, 1969 the first word spoken from the moon was Houston.

The largest rose garden in the world is the Tyler Municipal Rose Garden.

Lyndon B. Johnson National Historical Park and LBJ Ranch are in Johnson City. The Library and Museum of the 36th president is in Austin.

The first domed stadium in the world was the Astrodome in Houston.

King Ranch in Texas is larger than the state of Rhode Island.

Fort Worth Cultural District is called the "Museum Capital of the Southwest" and includes: The Museum of Science and History, Will Rogers Memorial Center, The Kimball Art, Modern Art and Amon Carter Museums.

More land is farmed in Texas than in any other state.

A nickle-iron meteorite made a ten acre depression near Odessa.

Capitan Reef at Guadalupe Mountains National Park is the most extensive fossil reef on record.

# UTAH

Utah:  The state of Utah was named for the Ute Indians.
Capital:  Salt Lake City
Flower:  Sego lily (*Calocortus nuttalli*) 1911
Tree:  Blue spruce (*Picea pungens*) 1933
Bird:  California gull (*Larus californicus*) 1955
Nickname:  The Beehive State
Rank:  45 (January 4, 1896)
Motto:  Industry 1959
Song:  Utah We Love Thee by Evan Stephens 1937
Folk Dance:  Square dance 1994
Gem:  Topaz 1969
Mineral:  Copper
Rock:  Coal 1991
Fossil:  Allosaurus or carnivorous theropod (*Allosaurus fragilis*), Jurassic 1988
Animal:  Rock mountain elk (*Cervus canadensis*) 1971
Insect:  Honeybee (*Apis mellifera*) 1983
Fish:  Bonneville cutthroat trout (*Onchorhynchus clarki utah*) 1997
Fruit:  Cherry 1997
Cooking Pot:  Dutch oven 1997
Grass:  Indian rice grass (*Oryzopsis hymenoides*) 1990
Emblem:  Beehive skep or domed hive of twisted straw 1959
Astronomical Symbol:  The beehive cluster located in the constellation of cancer the crab 1996

# HISTORY

Spanish explorers from the Coronado expedition visited the area in 1540.

In 1776 the region was explored for Spain by Silvestre Velez de Escalante and Francisco Atanasio Dominguez.

The Great Salt Lake was discovered in 1824 by James Bridger.

Joseph Smith founded the Church of Jesus Christ of Latter Day Saints in Fayette, New York in 1830. The church and its congregation became known as Mormon. The Mormon Church and its congregation were forced to move because their beliefs were opposed and believers were persecuted. In 1844 Joseph Smith and his brother Hyram were shot by a mob in Nauvoo, Illinois.

Brigham Young led the Mormons to the Great Salt Lake and founded Salt Lake City in 1847.

In 1849 the Mormons attempted to join the Union as the state of Deseret but were refused.

The region was admitted to the Union as the Territory of Utah in 1850.

In Little Cottonwood Canyon silver was discovered in 1868.

A golden spike was driven at Promontory Point on May 10, 1869 to commemorate the completion of the first transcontinental railroad.

The United States outlawed polygamy in 1862. The Mormons were forced into accepting monogamist laws by the Edmonds Bill which took citizenship away from polygamists. Polygamy was renounced by the church in 1890 when courts threatened to take Mormon Church property.

In 1952 uranium was discovered near Moab.

# FACTS AND TRIVIA

It took forty years to complete the Mormon Temple in Salt Lake City.

Deseret as mentioned in the Book of Mormon is interpreted as being a honeybee and is also associated with the beehive symbol.

Two thirds of the states population are Mormon.

Butch Cassidy the outlaw hid in the area of what is now Capitol Reef National Park in Torrey.

Topaz is the official state gem of Utah. Topaz Mountain is in the Thomas Mountain Range in Juab County. Topaz from the mountain fades when it is exposed to light so they have little commercial value.

The Great Salt Lake in Salt Lake City is the second largest salt lake in the world.

Temple Square in Salt Lake City is headquarters for the Mormon Church.

Utah, Colorado, Arizona and New Mexico join in the southeastern corner of Utah. It is the only place in the United States where four states join.

Natural wonders can be seen at Arches, Canyonlands, Capitol Reef, Bryce Canyon and Zion National Parks in Utah.

The longest natural stone arch in the world is thought to be Landscape Arch at Arches National Park in Moab.

Glen Canyon National Recreation Area was created by Glen Canyon Dam in Arizona.

# VERMONT

Vermont: Vermont is derived from the French words *verd mont* which
      mean green mountain.

Capital: Montpelier

Flower: Red clover (*Trifolium pratense*) 1894

Tree: Sugar maple (*Acer saccharum*) 1949

Bird: Hermit thrush (*Catharus guttatus*) 1941

Nickname: The Green Mountain State

Rank: 14 (March 4, 1791)

Motto: Freedom and unity

Song: Hail, Vermont by Josephine Hovey Perry
      These Green Mountains by Diane Martin and Rita Buglass 1999

Gemstone: Grossular garnet 1993

Minerals: Talc 1993

Rocks: Granite 1992
      Marble 1992
      Slate 1992

Fossil: White beluga whale or Charlotte whale (*Delphinapterus leucas*),
      Pleistocene 1993

Soil: Tunbridge soil series 1985

Animal: Morgan horse (*Equus caballus*) 1961

Insect: Honeybee (*Apis mellifera*) 1977

Butterfly: Monarch butterfly (*Danaus plexippus*) 1987

Amphibian: Northern leopard frog (*Rana pipiens*) 1997

Fishes: Brook trout (*Salvelinus fontinalis*) 1978
      Walleye pike (*Stizosedion vitreum*) 1978

Beverage: Milk 1983

Fruit: Apple (*Malus*) 1999

Pie: Apple pie 1999

Flavor: Maple Extracted from the Vermont sugar maple tree. 1993

Poet Laureate: Galway Kennell

Coat of Arms: Vermont Coat of Arms 1779

# HISTORY

The region was explored for France by Samuel de Champlain. He discovered Lake Champlain in 1609.

In 1666 La Motte Island in Lake Champlain was settled by the French.

Fort Drummer was built at Brattleboro by English colonists in 1724.

There were disputes over charter land grants made by both England and France. When the rights and claims of settlers who had purchased land from New Hampshire were ignored armed conflict resulted especially at Bennington.

The Green Mountain Boys were organized by Ethan Allen in 1764. Ethan Allen rid the state of New Yorkers in 1770.

During most of the War for Independence Vermont fought independently seeking an independent peace.

Fort Ticonderoga and Fort Crown Point were captured by Ethan Allen and his Green Mountain Boys in 1775.

The region called New Connecticut was renamed Vermont in 1777.

British General John Burgoyne was defeated by John Stark near Bennington in 1777.

Claims to the region were relinquished by: Massachusetts (1781), New Hampshire (1782) and New York (1790). Vermont joined the Union in 1791.

In 1814 a British fleet was defeated by Thomas MacDonough on Lake Champlain near Plattsburgh.

Vermont was given direct access to the port of New York in 1823 through a canal between the Hudson River and Lake Champlain.

Confederate soldiers stole 400,000 dollars from St. Albans bank in 1862.

The Blue Law was repealed in 1982 allowing stores to open on Sundays.

# FACTS AND TRIVIA

Vermont was the first state admitted to the Union after the thirteen original colonies. For 14 years statehood was bitterly opposed for Vermont because both New York and New Hampshire had claims on the land.

The smallest state capital in the country is Montpelier.

A statue of Ceres tops the gold dome of the state capitol building. Ceres was the Roman goddess of agriculture.

The largest city in Vermont is Burlington.

Montpelier is the largest producer of maple syrup in the United States. The Maple Sugar Museum is in St. Johnsbury.

At 4,393 feet Mt. Mansfield in Stowe is the highest peak in Vermont.

President Calvin Coolidge was born in Plymouth on July 4, 1872. He was the only president to be born on the fourth of July.

IBM is the largest employer in Vermont.

The Vermont Marble Exhibit, Norman Rockwell Museum and Calvin Coolidge Homestead are in Rutland.

Bennington was the first chartered town in Vermont.

The Revolutionary War Battle Monument, Museum and Art Gallery of Vermont is in Bennington.

# VIRGINIA

Virginia:  The state was named in 1584 for Queen Elizabeth I who was called the virgin Queen.

Capital:  Richmond

Flower:  American dogwood (*Cornus florida*) 1918

Tree:  American dogwood (*Cornus florida*) 1956

Bird:  Cardinal (*Cardinalis cardinalis*) 1950

Nickname:  Old Dominion, The Mother of Presidents, The Cavalier State or The Mother of States

Rank:  10 (June 25, 1788)

Motto:  *Sic Semper Tyrannis* (Thus ever to tyrants) 1776

Song:  Carry Me Back To Old Virginia by James Bland 1940

Folk Dance:  Square dance 1991

Fossil:  Extinct scallop (*Chesapecten jeffersonius*), Pliocene 1993

Shell:  Oyster shell (*Crassostraea virginica*) 1974

Dog:  American foxhound (*Canis lupis familiaris*) 1966

Insect:  Eastern tiger swallowtail butterfly (*Papilio glaucus*) 1991

Fish:  Brook trout (*Salvelinus fontinalis*) 1993

Beverage:  Milk 1982

Language:  English

Boat:  *Chesapeake Bay Deadrise* 1988

Folklore Center:  Blue Ridge Institute in Ferrum, Virginia 1986

Artisans Center:  Virginia Center in Waynesboro, Virginia

Historical Drama:  *The Long Way Home* staged by Earl Hobson Smith and performed in Radford, Virginia

Outdoor Drama:  *The Trail of the Lonesome Pine* staged by Clara Lou Kelly and performed in Big Stone Gap, Virginia

Sports Hall of Fame:  Virginia Sports Hall of Fame in Portsmouth, Virginia

Emergency Medical Services Museum:  To the Rescue in Roanoke, Virginia

Motor Sports Museum:  Wood Brothers Racing Museum and Virginia Motor Sports Hall of Fame in Patrick County

War Museum:  Virginia War Museum in Newport, Virginia

Salute:  Virginia flag salute 1954

Mace:  House of Delegates Mace  A ceremonial staff or rod carried as a symbol of office or authority which was presented to the House of Delegates by the Jamestown Foundation.  1974

# HISTORY

Under a charter issued by King James I in 1606 John Smith founded Jamestown in 1607. It was the first permanent settlement in North America.

In 1614 John Rolfe married Pocahontas. She was the daughter of Powhatan who was the Indian leader of the Powhatan Confederacy.

In Jamestown the first legislative assembly in the Western Hemisphere, the House of Burgesses convened in 1619.

In 1622 Indians massacred one third of the colonists in Jamestown.

The first resistance to taxation without representation was made in 1653 with the Northampton Declaration.

In 1693 the College of William and Mary was founded.

The Committee of Correspondence was established in 1773.

Royal Governor Dunmore fled when Virginians took over much of the government in 1775. George Washington was elected commander and chief on June 14, 1775. He took control of the army in Cambridge, Massachusetts.

Benedict Arnold the traitor burned Richmond and Petersburg for the British in 1781.

The American Revolution ended when British General Charles Cornwallis surrendered to George Washington at Yorktown in 1781.

Virginia ceded from the Union in 1861 and was readmitted in 1870.

Robert E. Lee surrendered to Ulysses S. Grant on April 9, 1865 at Appomattox Courthouse. His surrender marked the end of the Civil War.

Norfolk Naval Base was founded in 1917.

In 1927 John D. Rockefeller began restoration of Colonial Williamsburg.

The University of Richmond received a 50 million dollar donation from E. Claiborne Robins.

# FACTS AND TRIVIA

Jamestown was the first capital of Virginia. Richmond the present capital of Virginia was also the capital of the Confederacy.

Scotchtown, Patrick Henry's home during the Revolutionary War and St. Johns Church where he gave his liberty or death speech are both in Richmond.

Presidents George Washington, Thomas Jefferson, James Madison, James Monroe, William Harrison, John Tyler and Zachary Taylor were from Virginia.

Jamestown was founded for the production of silk. The silk worms food source, mulberry trees, were stricken with a blight fungus so the colonists decided to grow tobacco. Tobacco is still the major cash crop in Virginia.

Virginians wrote both the Declaration of Independence (Thomas Jefferson) and the model for the Bill of Rights (George Mason).

Presidents George Washington, Thomas Jefferson, James Madison, James Monroe, John Tyler, William Taft and John Kennedy are buried in Virginia.

The largest Confederate collection of artifacts in America is housed by the Museum and White House of the Confederacy in Richmond.

George Washington's plantation Mount Vernon overlooks the Potomac River in Alexandria. His boyhood home is in Fredericksburg.

# WASHINGTON

Washington:  The state of Washington was named in honor of George Washington the first President of the United States.

Capital:  Olympia

Flower:  Coast rhododendron (*Rhododendron macrophyllum*) 1892

Tree:  Western hemlock (*Tsuga heterophylla*) 1947

Bird:  American goldfinch (*Carduelis tristis*) 1951

Nickname:  The Evergreen State 1889

Rank:  42 (November 11, 1889)

Motto:  *Al-ki* or *Alki* (Indian word for by and by)

Song:  Washington, My Home by Helen Davis and Stuart Churchill 1959

Folk Song:  Roll On, Columbia, Roll On by Woody Guthrie 1987

Dance:  Square dance 1979

Gem:  Petrified wood, Tertiary 1975

Fossil:  Columbian woolly mammoth (*Mammuthus columbi*), Pleistocene 1998

Grass:  Bluebunch wheat grass (*Agropyron spicatum*) 1989

Insect:  Green darner dragonfly or mosquito hawk (*Anax junius drury*) 1997

Fish:  Steelhead trout (*Oncorhynchus mykiss ivideus*) 1969

Fruit:  Apple 1989

Ship:  *President Washington* 1983

Arboretum:  Washington Park Arboretum 1934

Tartan:  Cloth consisting of perpendicular bands of blue, white, yellow, red and black stripes on a green background.  1991

# HISTORY

Sir Francis Drake explored the coast of the pacific northwest in 1579.

In 1775 Bruno de Heceta sailed the coast and landed at Hoh River.

Captain James Cook visited the region in 1778.

The Columbia River was explored by Captain Robert Gray in 1792. The river was named for his ship the Columbia.

George Vancouver explored the Puget Sound in 1792.

In 1805 Meriwether Lewis and William Clark explored Columbia.

A protestant settlement was created by Marcus Whitman near Walla Walla in 1836.

In 1846 an agreement was made with Britain placing the border of Washington and Canada on the forty ninth parallel of latitude. Washington was then part of the future Oregon Territory.

Oregon Territory was formed in 1848 and in 1853 Washington Territory was separated from Oregon.

Gold was discovered in 1855 in northeastern Washington.

In 1883 the Northern Pacific Railroad reached the Puget Sound.

Grand Coulee Dam was completed in 1941. It is the largest concrete hydroelectric dam in the United States.

In 1974 Native Americans were awarded half the catch of northwest salmon and steelhead to uphold original territorial treaty provisions.

There were 60 people killed when Mount St. Helens erupted in 1980. Mount St. Helens in the Gifford Pinchot National Forest is a major attraction.

Washington apple growers lost 140 million dollars because of reports which linked the growth enhancing chemical Alar to cancer generation.

## FACTS AND TRIVIA

Washington produces more apples than any other state.

Microsoft Corporation the leading software company in the world is located in Redmond. Microsoft founder Bill Gates lives in Medina.

The longest floating bridge in the world is the Albert D. Rosellini bridge connecting Seattle and Medina across Lake Washington.

There is a replica of the prehistoric Stonehenge ruin in Maryhill.

Bill Speidels Underground Tour of Seattle explores a subterranean neighborhood that was created when the street level was raised 100 years ago.

Boeing's final assembly plant in Everett is the world's largest building.

An Apollo command module is displayed at the Museum of Flight at Boeing Field in Seattle.

The Space Needle at Seattle Center is 605 feet tall.

Klickitat Indians called Mount St. Helens *Tahonelatclah* which means fire mountain. A lava dome has formed in the crater of Mount St. Helens since its May 18, 1980 eruption.

Starbucks, the largest coffee chain in the world, was founded in Seattle.

At 14,410 feet Mount Rainier is the highest peak in the Cascade Mountains. There are over 300 miles of trails in Mount Rainer National Park.

# WEST VIRGINIA

West Virginia:  The state was named for Queen Elizabeth I who was called the virgin Queen.

Capital:  Charleston

Flower:  Big laurel (*Rhododendron maximum*) 1903

Tree:  Sugar maple (*Acer saccharum*) 1949

Bird:  Cardinal (*Cardinalis cardinalis*) 1949

Nickname:  The Mountain State

Rank:  35 (June 20, 1863)

Motto:  *Montani Semper Liberi* (Mountaineers are always free)

Songs:  The West Virginia Hills by Mrs. Ellen King and H. E. Engle 1963

This Is My West Virginia by Iris Bell 1963

West Virginia, My Home, Sweet Home by Julian G. Hearne, Jr. 1963

Gem:  Chalcedony, fossil or rugose coral (*Lithostrotionella*) 1990

Soil:  Monongahela silt loam 1997

Animal:  Black bear (*Ursus americanus*) 1955

Butterfly:  Monarch butterfly (*Danaus plexippus*) 1995

Fish:  Brook trout (*Salvelinus fontinalis*) 1973

Fruit:  Apple (*Malus*) 1972

Golden delicious apple (*Malus*) 1995

Colors:  Old gold and blue 1963

Day:  The 20th of June is West Virginia Day.  1927

# HISTORY

The first permanent settlement of the region was made in 1731 at Mill Creek by Morgan Morgan.

Coal was discovered on Coal River in 1742.

In 1753 George Washington explored the region.

George Washington set up the first national munitions factory at Harpers Ferry in the mid-1800's.

Antislavery revolutionary John Brown and 21 others raided the munitions factory at Harpers Ferry in 1859. Robert E. Lee and U. S. troops captured John Brown. He was convicted of treason in Charles Town and hung.

West Virginia was originally part of Virginia but objected to being ruled by the eastern part of the state so when Virginia seceded from the Union in 1861 the western counties seceded from Virginia. In 1861 the western counties formed the state of Kanahwa.

Union and Confederate soldiers fought the Battle of Philippe on June 3, 1861. It was the first major land battle fought in the Civil War.

The state joined the Union as West Virginia in 1863.

In 1926 the first federal prison in the United States exclusively for women was opened in West Virginia.

West Virginia has lead the nation in coal production since 1936.

From 1980-1983 unemployment in the state of West Virginia was the highest in the nation jumping from 8.6% to 18%.

## FACTS AND TRIVIA

Monongahela National Forest protects the 140 mile crest of the Allegheny Mountains. It is the most extensive wilderness area near the east coast.

A monument of black activist Booker T. Washington is on the grounds of the states capital building in Charleston.

Two thirds of the state is covered by the Allegheny Plateau.

John Brown Museum in Harpers Ferry details the raid that was conducted on the national munitions factory in 1859. At the Master Armorer's House in Harpers Ferry the art of gun making is explained.

West Virginia's state capitol building in Charleston completed in 1932 was designed by Lincoln Memorial architect Cass Gilbert.

Appalachian culture is renewed by the annual Augusta Festival in Elkins.

New River carved a 1,000 foot canyon through the mountains in West Virginia to form the spectacular river canyon called New River Gorge.

On Memorial Day weekend the annual Vandalia Festival is held in Charleston. The festival features bluegrass music, folk arts and local crafts.

West Virginia has been called the Ireland of the United States.

Berkeley Springs is known as the old spa town. The state runs the old Roman Baths which have been in active use since 1815.

One of the major chemical producing areas in the United States is the Kanawha Valley in West Virginia.

West Virginia is the youngest state east of the Mississippi River.

# WISCONSIN

Wisconsin:  Wisconsin is derived from the Ojibwa word *wishkonsing* which means place of the bearer.

Capital:  Madison

Flower:  Wood violet (*Viola papilionacea*) 1949

Tree:  Sugar maple (*Acer saccharum*) 1949

Bird:  American robin (*Turdus migratorius*) 1949

Nickname:  The Badger State

Rank:  30 (May 29, 1848)

Motto:  Forward

Song:  On Wisconsin by William T. Purdy 1959

Dance:  Polka 1993

Rock:  Red granite 1971

Mineral:  Galena (*Lead sulfide*) 1971

Fossil:  Trilobite or extinct arthropod (*Calymene celebra*), Silurian 1985

Soil:  Antigo silt loam 1983

Animal:  Badger (*Taxidea taxus*) 1957

Wildlife Animal:  White tailed deer (*Odocoileus virginianus*) 1957

Domestic Animal:  Dairy cow (*Bos taurus*) 1971

Dog:  American water spaniel (*Canis lupis familiaris*) 1985

Insect:  Honeybee (*Apis mellifera*) 1977

Fish:  Muskellunge or muskie (*Esox masquinongy*) 1955

Grain:  Corn (*Zea mays*) 1989

Beverage:  Milk 1987

Symbol of Peace:  Mourning dove (*Zenaida macroura*) 1971

# HISTORY

French Canadians explored the region which included Wisconsin.

In 1634 Jean Nicolet visited eastern Wisconsin.

Traders Radisson and Groseilliers explored the region in 1658.

Father Allouez established a mission in 1665 near Green Bay.

In 1670 the first permanent settlement was made near Green Bay.

Until the French were defeated in 1763 the state was part of New France.

In 1763 the British took control of the region. Early settlers retained allegiance to the English during the Revolutionary War.

The United States acquired the land as the result of the Treaty of Paris in 1783 and in 1787 the land was included in the Ordinance which established the Northwest Territory.

In 1800 Indiana Territory was separated from the Northwest Territory. Wisconsin was included in the Indiana Territory.

Wisconsin became part of Michigan Territory in 1805, Illinois Territory in 1808 and in 1818 Wisconsin was transferred back to Michigan Territory.

The region was controlled by the British until the War of 1812.

Wisconsin Territory was organized in 1838.

Statehood was achieved in 1848 and Wisconsin was reduced to its current boundaries.

In 1854 the Republican Party was founded in Ripon.

The first hydroelectric plant was completed at Appleton in 1882.

In 1911 Wisconsin became the first state to enact income tax.

# FACTS AND TRIVIA

Established in 1911 Devils Lake State Park in Baraboo is the oldest and most popular state park in Wisconsin.

Wisconsin leads the nation in the production of dairy products.

Tours are offered at Miller and Sprecher breweries in Milwaukee.

Milwaukee's Summerfest with an average of 2,500 performers is the largest music festival in the United States.

The Mustard Museum in Mount Horeb contains 2,300 types of mustard.

Monroe is the "Swiss Cheese Capital of the World".

The top tourist attraction in Wisconsin is the House on the Rock near Spring Green. Perched on a 60 foot chimney of rock it is an architectural marvel. Alex Jordan began construction of the natural rock structure in 1944.

Taliesin, architect Frank Lloyd Wright's home is south of Spring Green.

Escape artist and magician Harry Houdini was born in Appleton.

Hayward is home to the National Freshwater Fishing Hall of Fame. The building that houses the hall of fame is shaped like a muskie.

The Harley-Davidson engine plant in Milwaukee offers tours.

Ringling Brothers Circus was first staged in 1884 at Baraboo.

Twenty one of the Apostle Islands are designated as national lakeshore.

The largest iron ore docks and the tallest grain elevator in the world are in Superior, Wisconsin.

# WYOMING

Wyoming:  The name Wyoming is derived from the Delaware word *maugh-wau-wa-ma* meaning large plains or alternating mountains and valleys.

Capital:  Cheyenne

Flower:  Indian paintbrush (*Castilleja linariaefolia*) 1917

Tree:  Plains cottonwood (*Populus sargentii*) 1947 and 1961

Bird:  Western meadowlark (*Sturnella neglecta*) 1927

Nickname:  Big Wyoming, The Equality State or The Cowboy State

Rank:  44 (July 10, 1890)

Motto:  Equal rights

Song:  Wyoming by C. E. Winter and G. E. Knapp 1955

Gemstone:  Jade (*Nephrite*) 1967

Fossil:  Fresh water herring fossil (*Knightia*), Eocene 1987

Dinosaur:  Horned dinosaur (*Triceratops*), Cretaceous 1994

Mammal:  Bison (*Bison bison*) 1985

Reptile:  Horned toad (*Douglassi brevirostre*) 1993

Fish:  Cutthroat trout (*Oncorhynchus clarki*) 1987

Language:  English

Symbol:  The bucking horse

# HISTORY

The region was claimed for France in 1682.

In 1743 Canadian explorer Pierre Gaultier de Varennes, sieur de Verendrye explored the Wyoming Wind River region.

The U. S. acquired most of the region in the Louisiana Purchase of 1803.

John Colter explored the Yellowstone region in 1807.

Powder River was explored by Wilson Hunt in 1811.

In 1834 William Sublette and Robert Campbell made the first white settlement of Wyoming at Fort William which is now called Fort Laramie.

Fremont Peak in the Wind River Range was explored by John C. Fremont and Kit Carson in 1842.

Fort Bridger was settled by Mormons migrating to Utah in 1853.

Indian wars occurred in 1854 and 1866 following detachment massacres.

Gold was discovered in 1867.

In 1868 Wyoming Territory was organized from parts of Utah, Dakota and Idaho Territories.

Union Pacific railroad was completed across the state in 1869.

In 1869 Wyoming became the first state to grant women the right to vote.

Yellowstone the first national nature park in the world opened in 1872.

The first woman governor was Nellie Taylor Ross. In 1925 she was elected governor of Wyoming.

In 1951 Cheyenne became the site of the first Intercontinental Ballistic Missile Base.

Yellowstone Park fires destroyed 1.6 million acres of land in 1988.

# FACTS AND TRIVIA

Most of Yellowstone Park is in northwestern Wyoming. The park has about 250 active geysers including "Old Faithful". It also has numerous hot springs, Grand Canyon of the Yellowstone, wildlife and waterfalls.

Uranium output in Wyoming ranks second in the nation.

The bucking bronco on license plates in Wyoming is named "Old Steamboat" after a legendary bronco that could not be ridden.

Fort Laramie built in 1834 was the most important military post in the northern plains during the Indian wars.

The Buffalo Bill Museum in Cody has many artifacts of western America.

Almost three million people visit Yellowstone National Park and Grand Teton National Park each year.

Devils Tower National Monument in northeastern Wyoming is an 865 foot column remnant of a volcanic intrusion.

Wyoming is the least populous but the 9th largest state in the union.

Grand Teton National Park near Yellowstone features mountain climbing and a float trip down the Snake River.

Cheyenne Frontier Days is a nine day annual festival held in late July featuring chuck wagon races, concerts, air shows and parades. The largest outdoor rodeo in the world is also held in Cheyenne.

# NOTES

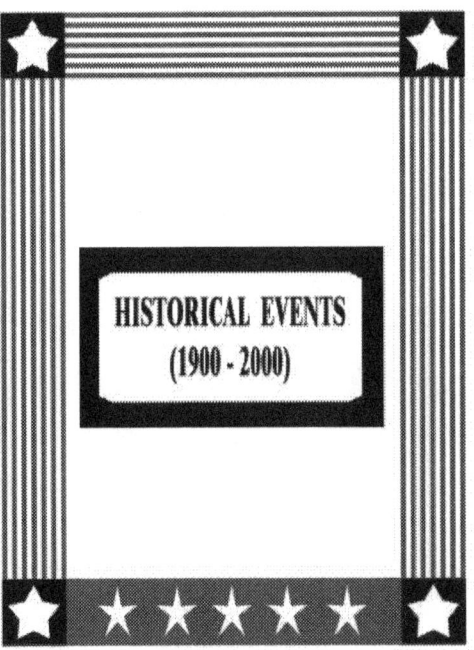

**HISTORICAL EVENTS**
**(1900 - 2000)**

# HISTORICAL EVENTS
## 1900 - 2000

1901 - President William McKinley was shot.

1903 - In Kitty Hawk, North Carolina the Wright Brothers flew the first airplane.

1904 - First ice cream cones were served at the St. Louis World's Fair.

1906 - Earthquake in San Francisco was 8.3 on the Richter scale.
First radio program.

1908 - Model T Automobile was produced by Henry Ford.
Plastic was invented.

1910 - Theory of Relativity was presented by Albert Einstein.
Boy Scouts of America was founded.

1912 - Titanic sunk.

1913 - Steamship Louise became the first ship to pass through the Panama Canal.
Zipper was patented by Gideon Sundback.
Girl Scouts was founded.

1914 - World War I began.

1917 - Communists took over Russia.
U. S. entered World War I.

1918 - Flu epidemic worldwide killed 20 million.

1919 - Germany was defeated in World War I.

1920 - Women were given the right to vote.
18th Amendment on prohibition passed.

1925 - First televised image was transmitted.

1928 - Penicillin was discovered by Alexander Fleming.

1927 - Charles Lindberg made the first solo flight across the Atlantic.
Academy Awards were first presented.

1928 - Amelia Earhart became the first woman to fly across the Atlantic.

1929 - Depression in U. S. began with the stock market crash.

1931 - Empire State Building in New York City opened.

1932 - Franklin D. Roosevelt was elected President.

1933 - Adolph Hitler took control of Germany.
Depression ended.

1937 - German airship Hindenberg crashed and burned.

1939 - First flight was made by a jet airplane.
World War II began when Germany invaded Poland.

1941 - U. S. entered World War II with Japanese attack on Pearl Harbor.
Television broadcasts began.

1945 - First electronic computer was demonstrated.
Atom bomb was tested in New Mexico.
Germany surrendered.
Japan surrendered after the U. S. dropped two atom bombs.

1947 - Rocket aircraft piloted by Chuck Yeager broke the sound barrier.

1947 - Brooklyn Dodgers signed Jackie Robinson. He was the first
       African-American major league baseball player.
1948 - Microwave oven was produced.
1950 - Korean War began. South Korea was defended by U. S. troops.
1951 - United States Census Bureau received Univac computer from
       Remington Rand.
1952 - Hydrogen bomb was created.
1953 - Polio vaccine was proven effective.
1955 - McDonald's restaurant opened.
1957 - First satellite Sputnik was launched by USSR.
1961 - First man in space was Russian Uri Gagarin.
       Alan Shepard became the first American in space.
1962 - First American to orbit the earth was John Glenn.
1963 - Russian Valentina Tereshkova was the first woman in space.
       President John F. Kennedy was assassinated in Dallas, Texas.
1964 - Vietnam War escalated.
       English musical group the Beatles were a success in the U. S.
       Civil Rights Act outlawed segregation.
1967 - First heart transplant was performed.
1968 - Martin Luther King, Jr. was killed in Memphis, Tennessee.
       Presidential candidate Robert F. Kennedy was killed in California.
1969 - American Neil Armstrong walked on the moon.
1973 - Last U. S. ground forces were withdrawn from Vietnam.
1974 - Illegal activities resulted in President Richard Nixon's resignation.
1975 - Saigon was taken over by the North Vietnamese.
       Microsoft was started by Bill Gates and Paul Allen.
1981 - AIDS was identified.
1986 - Space shuttle Challenger exploded killing seven astronauts.
       Chernobyl nuclear plant in Russia exploded killing 7,000.
1989 - Internet was improved by the World Wide Web.
1990 - Portable computers were developed.
       Space telescope Hubble was launched.
1991 - Persian Gulf War began with the invasion of Kuwait by Iraq.
       Dow Jones was above 3,000.
       USSR was dissolved.
1996 - Adult ewe cell was used to clone a lamb.
1997 - Septuplets were born to Bobbi McCaughey.
       Photos were sent by Pathfinder which landed on Mars.
1998 - President William Clinton was threatened with impeachment in
       sex scandal.
1999 - Dow Jones was above 11,000.
       John Glenn became the oldest American to be in space.
       Y2K bug concerned nation.
2000 - Votes are recounted in the George Bush and Al Gore presidential
       election. Abolition of the Electoral College is considered.

NATIONAL PARKS

# NATIONAL PARKS

ALABAMA - None.

ALASKA - **Denali National Park**
**Gates of the Arctic National Park**
**Glacier Bay National Park**
**Katmai National Park**
**Kenai Fjords National Park**
**Kobuk Valley National Park**
**Lake Clark National Park**
**Sitka National Historic Park \***
**Wrangell St. Elias National Park**

ARIZONA - **Grand Canuon National Park**, P. O. Box 129, Grand Canyon, AZ 86023. 602-638-7888.
**Petrified Forest National Park**, P. O. Box 2217, Petrified Forest, AZ 86028. 602-524-6228.

ARKANSAS - **Hot Springs National Park**, Hot Springs Convention & Visitors Bureau, P. O. Box K AR 71901. 800-543-BATH.

CALIFORNIA - **Channel Islands National Park**, 1901 Spinnaker Dr., Ventura, CA 93001. 805-658-5730.
**Death Valley National Park**, P. O. Box 579, Death Valley, CA 92328. 760-786-2331.
**Joshua Tree National Park**, 74485 National Park Drive,Twentynine Palms, CA 92277. 760-367-5500.
**Kings Canyon National Park**, Sequoia & Kings Canyon National Parks, P. O. Box 789, Three Rivers, CA 93271. 209-561-3314.
**Lassen Volcanic National Park**, P. O. Box 100, Mineral, CA 96063-0100. 916-595-4444.
**Redwood National Park**, 1111 Second St., Crescent City, CA 95531. 707-464-6101.
**Sequoia National Park**, Sequoia & Kings Canyon National Parks, P. O. Box 789, Three Rivers, CA 93271. 209-561-3314.
**Yosemite National Park**, P. O. Box 577, Yosemite, CA 95389. 209-372-0200.

COLORADO - **Mesa Verde National Park**, P. O. Box 8, CO 81330, 303-529-4421.
**Rocky Mountain National Park**, Estes Park, CO 89517-8397. 303-586-1206.

CONNECTICUT - None.
DELAWARE - None.

FLORIDA - **Biscayne National Park**, P. O. Box 1369, Homestead, FL 33090-1369. 305-230-1144.

**Dry Tortugas National Park.**, P. O. Box 6208, Key West, FL 33041.

**Everglades National Park**, 40001 State Road 9336, Home stead, FL 33034-6733. 305-242-7700.

GEORGIA - None.

HAWAII - **Haleakala National Park** (Maui).

**Hawaii Volcanoes National Park** (Hawaii).

IDAHO - None.

ILLINOIS - None.

INDIANA - None.

IOWA - None.

KANSAS - None.

KENTUCKY - **Mammoth Cave National Park**, Mammoth Cave, KY 42259. 502-758-2328.

LOUISIANA - None.

MAINE - **Acadia National Park**, P. O. Box 177, Bar Harbor, ME 04609. 207-288-0300.

MARYLAND - None.

MASSACHUSETTS - None.

MICHIGAN - **Isle Royale National Park**, 800 E. Lakeshore Dr., Houghton, MI 49931. 906-482-0984.

MINNESOTA - **Voyageurs National Park**, 3131 Hwy 53, International Falls, MN 56649. 218-283-9821.

MISSISSIPPI - None.

MISSOURI - None.

MONTANA - **Glacier National Park**, West Glacier, MT 59936. 406-888-5441.

NEBRASKA - None.

NEVADA - **Great Basin National Park**, Baker, NV 89311. 702-234-7331.

NEW HAMPSHIRE - None.

NEW JERSEY - None.

NEW MEXICO - **Carlsbad Caverns National Park**, 3225 National Parks Hwy., Carlsbad, NM 88220. 505-785-2233.

NEW YORK - None.

NORTH CAROLINA - None.

NORTH DAKOTA - **Theodore Roosevelt National Park**, P. O. Box 7, Medora, ND 58645. 701-623-4466.

OHIO - None.

OKLAHOMA - None.

OREGON - **Crater Lake National Park**, P. O. Box 7, Crater Lake, OR 97504. 503-594-221.

PENNSYLVANIA - None.

RHODE ISLAND - None.

SOUTH CAROLINA - None.

SOUTH DAKOTA - **Badlands National Park**, P. O. Box 6, Interior SD 57750. 605-433-5361.

**Wind Cave National Park**, RR 1 Box 190, Hot Springs, SD 57747. 605-745-4600.

TENNESSEE - **Great Smoky Mountains National Park**, 107 Park H. Q. Rd., Gattlinburg, TN 37738. 615-436-1200.

TEXAS - **Big Bend National Park**, P. O. Box 129, Big Bend, TX 79834. 915-477-2251.

**Guadalupe Mountains National Park**, HC60, P. O. Box 400, Salt Flat, TX 79847-9400. 915-828-3251.

UTAH - **Arches National Park**, P. O. Box 907, Moab, UT 84532. 801-259-8161.

**Bryce Canyon National Park**, Bryce Canyon, UT 84717. 801-834-5322.

**Capitol Reef National Park**, HC70 P. O. Box 15, Torrey, UT 84775-9602. 801-425-3791.

**Canyonlands National Park**, 2282 S. W. Resource Blvd., Moab, UT 84532-8000. 801-259-7164.

**Zion National Park**, Springdale, UT 84767-1099. 801-772-3256.

VERMONT - None.

VIRGINIA - **Shenandoah National Park**, Rt. 4, P. O. Box 348, Luray, VA 22835. 703-999-3483.

WASHINGTON - **Mount Rainier National Park**, Tahoma Woods, Star Route, Ashford, WA 98304-9751. 206-569-2211.

**North Cascades National Park**, 2105 Wash. Hwy 20, Sedro Woolley, WA 98284. 206-856-5700.

**Olympic National Park**, 600 East Park Ave., Port Angeles, WA 98362. 206-452-4501, EXT. 230.

WEST VIRGINIA - None.

WISCONSIN - None.

WYOMING - **Grand Teton National Park**, P. O. Drawer 170, Moose, WY 83012. 307-739-3300.

**Yellowstone National Park**, P. O. Box 168, Yellowstone National Park, WY 82190. 307-344-7381.

# NOTES

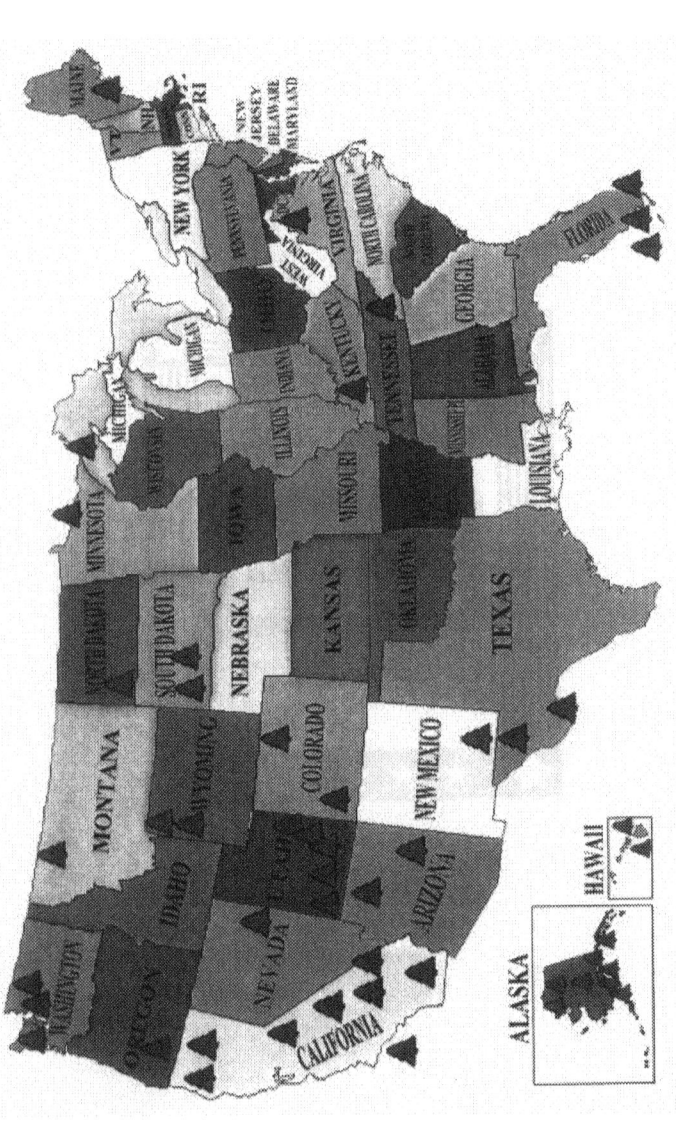

UNITED STATES NATIONAL PARKS

PLACES OF INTEREST

# PLACES OF INTEREST
## ALABAMA
Alabama Deep Sea Fishing Rodeo, Dauphin Island
Alabama Space and Rocket Center, U. S. Space Camp, Huntsville
Battleship USS Alabama, Mobile
Bellingrath Gardens, Theodore
Birmingham Museum of Art
First White House of the Confederacy, Montgomery
Horseshoe Bend National Military Park
Mound State Monument Archaeological Museum, Moundville
Museum of Natural History, University of Alabama, Tuscaloosa
Point Clear (resort)
Russel Cave National Monument
Tuskegee Institute
## ALASKA
Aniakchak National Monument
Cape Krusenstern National Monument
Denali National Park
Gates of the Arctic National Park
Glacier Bay National Park
Katmai National Park
Kenai Fjords National Park
Klondike Gold Rush National Park
Kobuk Valley National Park
Lake Clark National Park
Little Diomede Island
Sitka National Historical Park
St. Michaels Cathedral, Sitka
Wrangell-St. Elias National Park
## ARIZONA
Canyon de Chelly National Monument
Casa Grande Ruins National Monument
Chiricahua National Monument
Ft. Bowie
Grand Canyon National Park
Heard Museum, Phoenix
London Bridge, Lake Havasu City
Montezuma Castle National Monument
Painted Desert
Petrified Forest National Park
Pipe Spring National Monument
Saguaro National Monument
Sunset Crater National Monument
Tallesin West, near Scottsdale

Tonto National Monument
Tumacacori National Monument
Tuzigoot National Monument
Walnut Canyon National Monument
Wupatki National Monument.

## ARKANSAS

Arkansas Post National Monument
Buffalo National River
Crater of Diamonds State Park, Murfeesboro
Eureka Springs
Ft. Smith National Historic Site
Hot Springs National Park
Pea Ridge National Military Park

## CALIFORNIA

Big Sur, Monterey
Cabrillo National Monument
California Academy of Sciences, San Francisco
California Palace of the Legion of Honor, San Francisco
Channel Islands National Park
Devils Postpile National Monument
Death Valley National Monument
Disneyland
Fine Arts Museum of San Francisco
Fishermens Wharf, San Francisco
Hollywood
Huntington Library and Botanical Gardens, San Marino
J. Paul Getty Museum, Malibu
Joshua Tree National Monument
Kings Canyon National Park
Lassen Volcanic National Park
Lava Beds National Monument
Los Angeles Co. Museum of Art
Muir Woods National Monument
Mt. Palomar Observatory
National Maritime Museum, San Francisco
Natural History Museum of Los Angeles
Natural History Museum of San Diego
Norton Simon Museum of Art at Pasadena
Pinnacles National Monument
Redwood National Park
Rosicrucian Egyptian Museum, San Jose
San Diego Museum of Art
San Diego Museum of Man
San Diego Zoo
San Francisco Museum of Modern Art

Sequoia National Park
Southwest Museum, Los Angeles
Yosemite National Park

## COLORADO

Black Canyon of the Gunnison National Monument
Buffalo Bill grave site, Evergreen
Central City Opera House
Colorado Springs Fine Arts Center
Denver Art Museum
Denver Mint
Denver Museum of Natural History
Dinosaur National Monument
Florissant Fossil Beds National Monument
Garden of the Gods, Colorado Springs
Great Sand Dunes National Monument
Hovenweep National Monument
Mesa Verde National Park
Molly Brown House, Denver
Pikes Peak
Red Rocks Amphitheater
Rocky Mountain National Park, Aspen
U. S. Air Force Academy, Colorado Springs
U. S. Olympic Headquarters, Colorado Springs
Yucca House National Monument

## CONNECTICUT

Charles Ives Center, Danbury
Eugene O'Neill Memorial Theater Center, Waterford
Gilette Castle
Housatonic State Park
Mark Twain House, Hartford
Mystic Marine life Aquarium
Mystic Seaport
Norwalk Maritime Center
U. S. Coast Guard Academy
*USS Nautilus*, New London
Wadsworth Atheneum, Hartford
Whitney Museum of Modern Art, Stamford
Yale Center for British Art, New Haven
Yale University, New Haven

## DELAWARE

Brandywine Zoo, Wilmington
Delaware Art Museum, Wilmington
Delaware State Museum, Dover
Dover Downs International Speedway
Grand Opera House, Wilmington

Hagley Museum, Wilmington
Rehoboth Beach

## FLORIDA

Biscayne National Park
Castillo de San Marcos, St. Augustine
Everglades National Park
Florida State Museum, Gainesville
Ft. Jefferson National Monument
Ft. Matanzas National Monument
Kennedy Space Center
Cape Canaveral
Ringling Museum, Sarasota
St. Augustine
Walt Disney World / EPCOT Center, Orlando

## GEORGIA

Chickamauga and Chattanooga National Military Park
Confederate Memorial, Stone Mountain
Ft. Frederica National Monument
Ft. Pulaski National Monument
High Museum of Art, Atlanta
Martin Luther King National Historic Site, Atlanta.
Ocmulgee National Monument
Okefenokee Swamp
Savannah Historic District

## HAWAII

Bernice P. Bishop Museum, Honolulu
Diamond Head
Haleakala National Park, Maui
Hawaii Volcanoes National Park, Hawaii
Iolani Palace, Honolulu
Kaloko-Honokohau National Historic Park, Molokai
National Cemetery of the Pacific and *USS Arizona* Memorial
Polynesian Cultural Center, Laiea
Pu'uhonua o Honaunau National Historic Park, Hawaii

## IDAHO

Craters of the Moons National Monument
Hell's Canyon National Recreation Area
Nez Perce National Historic Park
Sawtooth National Recreation Area
Sun Valley ski resort
Yellowstone National Park

## ILLINOIS

Art Institute of Chicago
Crab Orchard Wildlife Refuge
Dickson Mounds Museum, Lewistown

Field Museum of Natural History, Chicago
Ft. Chartres
Ft. Kaskaskia
Ft. Massac
Frank Lloyd Wright Historic District, Oak Park
Illinois State Museum, Springfield
Lincoln Home National Historic Park, Springfield
Mormon Settlement, Nauvoo
Morton Arboretum, Lisle
Museum of Science and Industry, Chicago
Shawnee National Forest
Starved Rock State Park

## INDIANA

Ernie Pyle birthplace, Dana
George Rogers Clark National Historic Park, Vincennes
Benjamin Harrison home, Indianapolis
Hoosier National Forest
Indiana Dunes National Lakeshore
Indianapolis Motor Speedway and Museum
Indianapolis Museum of Art
New Harmony village
Notre Dame University, South Bend
Old state capital, Corydon
Wilbur Wright State Memorial, Millville
Wyandotte Cave
Tippecanoe sites

## IOWA

Amana Colonies
Davenport Art Gallery
Des Moines Art Center
Effigy Mounds National Monument, Marquette
Ft. Dodge Historical Museum
Herbert Hoover birthplace and library, West Branch
National Rivers Hall of Fame, Dubuque
Putnam Museum, Davenport

## KANSAS

Agricultural Hall of Fame, Kansas City
Dodge City
Eisenhower Center, Abilene
Ft. Larned
Ft. Leavenworth
Ft. Riley
Ft. Scott
John Brown's Cabin, Osawatomie
Kansas Cosmosphere and Space Discovery Center, Hutchinson

Kansas State Historical Society Museum, Topeka
Wichita Art Museum
## KENTUCKY
Abraham Lincoln birthplace, Hodgenville
Churchill Downs, Louisville
George S. Patton, Jr Military Museum, Fort Knox
J. B. Speed Art Museum, Louisville
Land Between the Lakes National Recreation Area
Mammoth Cave National Park
My Old Kentucky Home, Bardstown
Old Ft. Harrod State Park
## LOUISIANA
Avery Island
Cabildo, New Orleans
French Quarter, New Orleans
Garden District, New Orleans
Hodges Gardens, Natchitoches
Jean Lafitte National Historic Park, Chalmette
Kent House Museum , Alexandria
Longfellow-Evangeline State Commemorative Area, St. Martinsville
Louisiana Maritime Museum, Baton Rouge
New Orleans Museum of Art
## MAINE
Acadia National Park, Mt. Desert Island
Allagash National Wilderness Waterway
Boothbay Railway Museum
Campobello-Longfellow House, Portland
Maine Maritime Museum, Bath
Portland Art Museum
Roosevelt-Campobello International Park, Campobello Island
St. Croix Island National Monument
## MARYLAND
Aberdeen Proving Ground
Antietam National Battlefield, Sharpsburg
Assateague Island National Seashore
National Aquarium in Baltimore
Baltimore Museum of Art
Baltimore Museum of Industry
Calvert Marine Museum, Solomons
Chesapeake & Ohio Canal National Historic Park
Chesapeake Bay Maritime Museum, St. Michaels
Ft. McHenry National Monument, Baltimore
Harpers Ferry National Historic Park
Liberty ship *John W. Brown*, Baltimore
St. Marys City

State House, Annapolis
U. S. Naval Academy, Annapolis
*USS Constellation*, Baltimore
Walters Art Gallery, Baltimore

## MASSACHUSETTS

Addison Gallery of American Art, Andover
Arnold Arboretum, Boston
Arthur M. Sackler Museum, Cambridge
Berkshires Museum, Pittsfield
Boston Museum of Fine Arts
Boston National Historic Park
Busch-Reisinger Museum, Cambridge
Cape Cod National Seashore
Clark Art Institute, Williamsburg
Fogg Art Museum, Boston
Gardner Art Museum, Boston
Lowell National Historic Park
Minute Man National Historic Park, Lexington and Concord
Nantucket Historic Society
Old Sturbridge
Peabody Museum, Salem
Plimoth Plantation, Plymouth
Shaker Village
Tanglewood Music Festival, Lenox
*USS Constitution*, Charlestown
Walden Pond
Woods Hole Oceanographic Institute
Worcester Art Museum

## MICHIGAN

Detroit Historical Society
Detroit Institute of Arts
Dossin Great Lakes Museum, Detroit
Great Lakes Indian Interpretive Museum, Detroit
Greenfield Village, Dearborn
Historic Ft. Wayne, Detroit
Isle Royale National Park
Mackinac Island
Pictured Rocks National Lakeshore, Lake Superior
Sleeping Bear Dunes National Lakeshore, Lake Superior

## MINNESOTA

Boundary Waters Canoe Area
Grand Portage National Monument
International Falls
Lake Itasca State Park
Mayo Clinic, Rochester

Minneapolis Institute of Arts
Minnehaha Falls, Minneapolis
Minnesota Zoo, Apple Valley
Pipestone National Monument
Tyrone Guthrie Theater, Minneapolis
Voyageurs National Park
Walker Art Center, Minneapolis

## MISSISSIPPI

Delta Blues Museum, Clarksdale
Natchez Trace National Parkway
Seafood Industry Museum, Biloxi
Tupelo National Battlefield
Vicksburg National Military Park

## MISSOURI

Churchill Memorial, St. Aldermanbury Church, Fulton
Gateway Arch, St. Louis
George Washington Carver National Monument, Diamond
Harry S. Truman Library, Independence
Mark Twain Area, Hannibal
Nelson-Atkins Museum of Art, Kansas City
Pony Express Museum, St. Joseph
St. Louis Art Museum
Wilson's Creek National Battlefield

## MONTANA

Big Hole National Battlefield
Bob Marshall Wilderness
Charles M. Russell Museum, Great Falls
Custer Battlefield National Monument
Ft. Union Trading Post National Historic Site
Lewis and Clark Caverns State Park
Museum of the Plains Indian, Browning
National Bison Range
Waterton-Glacier International Peace Park
World Museum of Mining, Butte
Yellowstone National Park

## NEBRASKA

Agate Fossil beds National Monument
Arbor Lodge State Park, Nebraska City
Boys Town, Omaha
Buffalo Bill Ranch State Historic Park
Chimney Rock Historic Site
Homestead National Monument, Beatrice
Oregon Trail
Pioneer Village, Minden
Scotts Bluff National Monument

Stuhr Museum of the Prairie Pioneer, Grand Island
## NEVADA
Death Valley National Monument
Lehman Caves National Monument
Valley of the Fire State Park, Overton
## NEW HAMPSHIRE
Currier Gallery of Art, Manchester
The Flume
Franconia Notch
Isles of Shoals
Lake Winnipesaukee
Mt. Washington
Shaker Village, Canterbury
St. Gaudens National Historic Site
Strawberry Bank
White Mountains National Forest
## NEW JERSEY
Cape May Historic District
Edison National Historic Site, West Orange
Lakehurst Naval Air Station
Liberty State Park, Jersey City
Morristown National Historic Park
Newark Museum
Palisades Interstate Park
Pine Barrens wilderness area
Princeton University
Walt Whitman House, Camden
## NEW MEXICO
Aztec Ruins National Monument
Bandelier National Monument
Capulin Mt. National Monument
Carlsbad Caverns National Park
Chaco Culture National Historic Park
El Morro National Monument
Ft. Union National Monument
Gila Cliff Dwellings National Monument
Museum of New Mexico, Santa Fe
Pecos Mission
Salinas Mission
Santa Fe Opera
Wheelwright Museum of the American Indian, Santa Fe
White Sands National Monument
## NEW YORK
Albright-Knox Gallery of American Art, Buffalo
American Merchant Marine Museum, Kings Point

Baseball Hall of Fame, Cooperstown
Bear Mt. State Park
Buffalo Museum of Science
Corning Glass Center, Corning
Erie Canal Museum, Syracuse
Farmers Museum, Cooperstown
Fenimore House, Cooperstown
Franklin D. Roosevelt National Historic Site, Hyde Park
Ft. Stanwix National Monument, Rome
Ft. Ticonderoga
Hudson Valley
Mohawk Valley
Niagara Falls
Palisades Interstate Park
Saratoga National Historic Park
Vanderbilt Museum, Hyde Park
U. S. Military Academy, West Point
Women's Rights National Historic Park, Seneca Falls

**New York City**
American Academy of Arts & Sciences
American Museum of Natural History
Bronx Zoo
Brooklyn Botanical Garden
Brooklyn Museum
Cathedral of St. John the Divine
Cooper-Hewitt Museum
Federal Hall
Fraunces Tavern
Frick Collection
Gugggenheim Museum
Hispanic Society of America
Jewish Museum
Lincoln Center for the Performing Arts
Metropolitan Museum of Art
Museum of Modern Art
Museum of the American Indian
N. Y. Public Library
N. Y. Stock Exchange
Rockefeller Center
South Street Seaport Museum
Statue of Liberty
United Nations

## NORTH CAROLINA

Bennett Place
Blue Ridge National Parkway

Cape Hatteras and Cape Lookout National Seashore
Carl Sandburg home, Hendersonville
Ft. Raleigh
Great Smoky Mountains National Historic Park
Guilford Courthouse National Military Park
Mint Museum, Charlotte
Moores Creek National Battlefield
North Carolina Maritime Museum, Beaufort
North Carolina Museum of Art, Raleigh
Roanoke Island
Wright Brothers National Memorial, Kitty Hawk

## NORTH DAKOTA

Ft. Abraham Lincoln State Park
Ft. Union Trading Post National Historic Site
International Peace Garden
Knife River Indian Villages National Historic Site
Theodore Roosevelt National Park, the Badlands

## OHIO

Air Force Museum, Dayton
Cleveland Museum of Art
Cleveland Museum of Natural History
Columbus Museum of Art
Great Lakes Historical Society Museum, Vermilion
Mound City Group National Monument, Chillicothe
Neil Armstrong Air and Space Museum, Wapakoneta
Ohio River Museum, Marietta
Pro Football Hall of Fame, Canton
Toledo Museum of Art

## OKLAHOMA

American Indian Hall of Fame, Anadarko
Chisholm Trail Museum, Kingfisher
Ft. Gibson Stockade, Muskogee
National Cowboy Hall of Fame, Oklahoma City
Ouachita National Forest
Pioneer Woman Museum, Ponca City
Will Rogers Memorial, Claremore

## OREGON

Bonneville Dam, Columbia River
Columbia River Gorge
Columbia River Museum, Astoria
Crater Lakes National Park
Ft. Clatsop National Monument
Hells Canyon
High Desert Museum, Bend
John Day Fossil Beds National Monument

Mt. Hood
Oregon Caves National Monument
Oregon Dunes National Recreation Area
Point Perpetua
Timberline Lodge

## PENNSYLVANIA

Academy of Natural Sciences, Philadelphia
Carnegie Institute, Pittsburgh
Delaware Water Gap National Recreation Area
Ft. Necessity National Battlefield
Franklin Institute, Philadelphia
Gettysburg Battlefield
Hugh Moore Historic Park and Museums, Easton
Independence National Historic Park, Philadelphia
Liberty Bell, Carpenters Hall, Philadelphia
Pennsylvania Academy of Fine Arts, Philadelphia
Pennsylvania Dutch Country
Philadelphia Museum of Art
Pine Creek Gorge
Valley Forge National Historic Park

## RHODE ISLAND

John Carter Brown Library, Providence
First Baptist Church in North America, Providence
Nathanael Greene homestead, Coventry
Hoffenreffer Museum of Anthropology, Bristol
Museum of Art of the Rhode Island School of Design, Providence
Newport mansions
Museum of Yachting, Newport
Tennis Hall of Fame, Newport
Touro Synagogue, Newport
Brown University, Providence

## SOUTH CAROLINA

Charleston Museum
Congaree Swamp National Monument
Cowpens National Battlefield
Ft. Moultrie
Ft. Johnson
Ft. Sumter National Monument, Charleston
Hilton Head Island
Kings Mountain National Military Park
Ninety Six National Historic Site, Greenwood
Patriots Point Maritime Museum, Charleston
Sea Islands
Spoleto Music Festival, Charleston

## SOUTH DAKOTA

Badlands National Park
Crazy Horse State Memorial, Custer
Custer State Park
Ft. Sisseton
Geographical center of the United States
Jewel Cave National Monument
Mount Rushmore National Memorial
Wind Cave National Park

## TENNESSEE

American Museum of Science and Energy, Oak Ridge
Andrew Johnson National Historic Site, Greenville
Chickamauga and Chattanooga National Military Park
Cumberland National Historic Park
Ft. Donelson National Military Park
Grand Old Opry, Nashville
Great Smoky Mountains National Park
The Hermitage, Nashville
Lookout Mountain, Chattanooga
The Parthenon, Nashville
Shiloh National Military Park, Pittsburgh Landing
Stones River National Battlefield, Murfreesboro

## TEXAS

The Alamo, San Antonio
Alibates Flint Quarries National Monument
Big Bend National Park
Ft. Davis
Galveston Historical Foundation
Guadalupe Mountains National Park
Houston  Museum of Fine Arts
Lyndon B. Johnson National Historic Park, Johnson City
Lyndon B. Johnson Space Center, Houston
Old Stone Ft., Nacogdoches
Padre Island National Seashore
San Antonio Missions National Historic Park
Texas Ranger Museum, Waco

## UTAH

Arches National Park
Bryce Canyon National Park
Canyonlands National Park
Capitol Reef National Park
Cedar Breaks National Monument
Dinosaur National Monument
Flaming Gorge Dam National Monument
Great Salt Lake

Lake Powell National Monument
Monument Valley
Mormon Tabernacle, Salt Lake City
Natural Bridges National Monument
Promontory Point
Rainbow Bridge National Monument
Temple Square, Salt Lake City
Timpanogas Cave National Monument
Zion National Park

## VERMONT

Bennington Battleground Monument
Calvin Coolidge Homestead, Plymouth
Maple Grove Maple Museum
Rock of Ages Tourist Center, Graniteville
Shelburne Museum
St. Johnsbury
Vermont Marble Exhibit, Proctor

## VIRGINIA

Appomattox Courthouse National Historic Park
Arlington National Cemetery
Booker T. Washington National Monument, Roanoke
Colonial National Historic Park
Fredericksburg and Spotsylvania National Military Park
George Washington Birth Place, Frederick County
Harpers Ferry National Historic Site
The Mariners Museum, Newport News
Monticello, Charlottesville
Mount Vernon
Petersburg National Battlefield
Robert E. Lee Memorial, Lexington
Shenandoah National Park
Virginia Beach
Virginia Museum of Fine Arts
Wolf Trap Farm for the Performing Arts, Reston

## WASHINGTON

Klondike Gold Rush National Historic Park, Seattle
Mount Rainier National Park
Mount Saint Helens National Monument
North Cascades National Park
Olympic National Park
San Juan Islands National Historic Park
Seattle Art Museum

## WASHINGTON (DISTRICT OF COLUMBIA)

The Capitol
Chesapeake & Ohio Canal National Historic Park

124

Corcoran Gallery of Art
Dumbarton Oaks
FDR Memorial
Folger Shakespeare Library
Freer Gallery of Art
Hirshhorn Museum
Jefferson Memorial
Kennedy Center
Korean War Veterans Memorial
Library of Congress
Lincoln Memorial
National Air and Space Museum
National Gallery of Art
National Museum of African Art
National Museum of American Art
National Museum of American History
National Museum of Natural History
National Portrait Gallery
Naval Observatory
Navy Memorial Museum
Renwick Gallery
Smithsonian Institution
Vietnam Veterans Memorial
Washington Monument
Washington Zoo
White House
Woodrow Wilson House

## WEST VIRGINIA

Cass Scenic Railroad
Harpers Ferry National Historic Park
Monongahela National Forest
New River Gorge Bridge
Science and Cultural Center, Charleston

## WISCONSIN

Apostle Island National Lakeshore
Chequamegon National Forest
Circus World Museum, Baraboo
Door County Peninsula
Ice Age National Scientific Reserve
Manitowoc Maritime Museum
Milwaukee Art Museum
Milwaukee Public Museum
Nicolet National Forest
Old Wade House and Carriage Museum, Greenbush
Old World Wisconsin, Eagle

Ville Louis, Prairie Du Chien
Wisconsin Dells

## WYOMING

Buffalo Bill Museum, Cody
Devil's Tower National Monument
Ft. Bridger State Park
Ft. Laramie National Historic Site
Fossil Butte National Monument
Grand Teton National Park
National Elk Refuge
Yellowstone National Park

TOURIST INFORMATION

# TOURIST INFORMATION

ALABAMA: Bureau of Tourism and Travel, 401 Adams Avenue, P. O. Box 4309, Montgomery, AL 36103-4309. 800-ALABAMA or 205-242-4169.

ALASKA: Division of Tourism, P. O. Box 110801, Juneau, AK 99811-0801. 907-465-2010.

ARIZONA: Office of Tourism, 1100 W. Washington St., Phoenix, AZ 85007. 800-842-8257. 602-542-8687.

CALIFORNIA: Department of Tourism, 801 K. Street, Suite 1600, Sacramento, CA 95814. 800-862-2543 or 916-322-1396.

COLORADO: Colorado Tourism Board, 1625 Broadway, Suite 1700, Denver, CO 80202. 800-265-6723 or 303-592-5410.

CONNECTICUT: Department of Tourism, 865 Brook Street, Rocky Hill, CT 06067. 800-CT-BOUND or 203-258-4355.

DELAWARE: Tourism Office, Box 1401, Dover, DE 19903. 800-441-8846.

DISTRICT OF COLUMBIA: Convention and Visitors Association, 1455 Pennsylvania Avenue N. W., Washington, D. C. 20004. 202-789-7038.

FLORIDA: Division of Tourism, 126 W. Van Buren St., Tallahassee, FL 32399-2999. 888-735-2872.

GEORGIA: Department of Industry, Trade and Tourism, P. O. Box 1776, Atlanta, GA 30301. 800-VISITGA.

HAWAII: Hawaii Visitors Bureau, 2270 Kalakaua Ave. Suite 801, Honolulu, HI 96815. 808-923-1811.

IDAHO: Department of Commerce, Tourism Development Division, 700 W. State St., Joe R. Williams Bldg, 2nd Floor, Boise, ID 83270-0093. 800-635-7820 or 208-334-2470.

ILLINOIS: Office of Tourism, General Information. 800-223-0121.

INDIANA: Department of Commerce, Tourism Development Division, One North Capitol, Suite 700, Indianapolis, IN 46204-2288. 800-289-6646 OR 317-232-8860.

IOWA: Department of Economic Development, 200 E. Grand Avenue, Des Moines, IA 50309. 800-345-IOWA or 515-242-4705.

KANSAS: Travel and Tourism Division, 700 S. W. Harrison, Suite 1300, Topeka, KS 66603-3712. 800-2KANSAS or 913-296-2009.

KENTUCKY: Department of Travel Development, 2200 Capital Plaza Tower, 500 Mero St. Frankfort, KY 40601. 800-225-8747 or 502-564-4930.

LOUISIANA: Office of Tourism, Department of Culture, Recreation and Tourism, P. O. Box 94291, 1501 N. 3rd, Baton Rouge, LA 70804-9291. 800-33GUMBO or 504-342-8100.

MAINE: Publicity Bureau, P. O. Box 2300, Halowell, ME 04347. 800-533-9595 or 207-582-9300.

MARYLAND: Office of Tourism Development, 217 E. Redwood St. Baltimore, MD 21202. 800-543-1036.

MASSACHUSETTS: Office of Travel and Tourism, 100 Cambridge St. 13th Floor, Boston, MA 02202. 800-447-MASS Ext. 500 or 617-727-3201.

MICHIGAN: Travel Bureau, Department of Commerce, P. O. Box 3393, Livonia, MI 48451-3393. 800-543-2YES or 517-373-1837.

MINNESOTA: Office of Tourism, 100 Metro Sq., 121 E. 7th Place, St. Paul, MN 55101-2112. 800-657-3700 or 612-296-5029.

MISSISSIPPI: Division of Tourism, P. O. Box 849, Jackson, MS 39205-0849. 800-927-6378 or 601-359-3297.

MISSOURI: Division of Tourism, P. O. Box 1055, Jefferson City, MO 65102. 800-877-1234 or 314-751-4133.

MONTANA: Travel Promotion Division, Department of Commerce, 1424 9th Avenue, Helena, MT 59620. 800-VISITMT or 406-444-2654.

NEBRASKA: Department of Economic Development, Division of Travel and Tourism, P. O. Box 94666, Lincoln, NE 68509. 800-228-4307 or 800-426-6505.

NEVADA: Department of Tourism, Capitol Complex, Carson City, NV 89710. 800-NAVADA8.

NEW HAMPSHIRE: Office of Travel and Tourism, P. O. Box 1856, Concord, NH 03302-1856. 800-258-3608 or 603-271-2343.

NEW JERSEY: Division of Travel and Tourism, CN 826,Trenton, NJ 08625. 800-JERSEY7.

NEW MEXICO: Tourism Department, 491 Old Santa Fe Trail, Lanie Bldg, Santa Fe, NM 87503. 800-545-2070 or 505-827-7400.

NEW YORK: Department of Economic Development, Division of Tourism, One Commerce Plaza, Albany, NY 12245. 800-CALLNYS or 518-474-4116.

NORTH CAROLINA: Travel and Tourism Division, 430 N Salisbury St., Raleigh, NC 27611. 800-847-4862 or 919-733-4171.

NORTH DAKOTA: Tourism Division, 600 E. Boulevard Avenue, Liberty Memorial Building, State Capitol Grounds, Bismarck, ND 58505. 800-435-5663 or 701-224-2525.

OHIO: Department of Development, Division of Travel and Tourism, P. O. Box 1001, Columbus, OH 43266-0101. 800-282-5393 or 614-466-8844.

OKLAHOMA: Tourism and Recreation Department, 500 Will Rogers Building, Oklahoma City, OK 73105-4492. 800-654-8240 or 405-521-2401.

OREGON: Economic Development Department, Tourism Division, 775 Summer St. N. E. Salem, OR 97310. 800-547-7842 or 503-378-3451.

PENNSYLVANIA: Department of Commerce, Office of Travel Marketing, 453 Forum Building, Harrisburg, PA 17120. 800-VISITPA or 717-787-5453.

RHODE ISLAND: Tourism Division, 7 Jackson Walkway, Providence, RI 02903. 800-556-2484 or 401-277-2601.

SOUTH CAROLINA: Division of Tourism, 1205 Pendleton Street, Columbia, SC 29201. 800-346-3634 or 803-734-0122.

SOUTH DAKOTA: Department of Tourism, Capitol Lake Plaza, 711 E.

SOUTH DAKOTA: Department of Tourism, Capitol Lake Plaza, 711 E. Wells Avenue, Pierre, SD 57501. 800-732-5682 or 605-773-3301.

TENNESSEE: Department of Tourist Development, Box 23170, Nashville, TN 37202-3170. 615-741-2158.

TEXAS: Texas Department of Transportation, Travel and Information Division P. O. Box 5064, Austin, TX 78701. 800-452-9292 or 512-463-8586.

UTAH: Travel Council, Council Hall/Capitol Hill, Salt Lake City, UT 84114. 801-538-1030 or 800-200-1160.

VERMONT: Department of Travel and Tourism, 134 State Street, Montpeiler, VT 05602. 800-VERMONT or 800-338-0189.

VIRGINIA: Division of Tourism, 1021 E. Cary Street, 14th Floor, Richmond, VA 23219. 800-VISITVA or 804-786-4484.

WASHINGTON: Tourism Development Division, Department of Trade and Economic Development, P. O. Box 42500, Olympia, WA 98504-2500. 800-544-1800 or 206-753-5630.

WEST VIRGINIA: Division of Tourism and Parks, State Capitol Complex, Charleston, MV 25305-0317. 800-CALLWVA or 304-558-2766.

WISCONSIN: Division of Tourism, P. O. Box 7606, Madison, WI 53707-7606. 800-432-TRIP or 608-266-2161.

WYOMING: Division of Tourism and State Marketing, I-25 at College Drive, Cheyenne, WY 82002. 800-225-5996 or 307-777-7777.

# IMPORTANT NUMBERS

## AIRLINES
American Airlines . . . . . . . . . . . . . . . . . . . . . . . . . . . . 800-433-7300
Continental . . . . . . . . . . . . . . . . . . . . . . . . . . . . . . . . .800-525-0280
Delta . . . . . . . . . . . . . . . . . . . . . . . . . . . . . . . . . . . . . .800-221-1212
Northwest . . . . . . . . . . . . . . . . . . . . . . . . . . . . . . . . . 800-225-2525
Southwest . . . . . . . . . . . . . . . . . . . . . . . . . . . . . . . . . 800-435-9792
TWA . . . . . . . . . . . . . . . . . . . . . . . . . . . . . . . . . . . . . .800-221-2000
USAir . . . . . . . . . . . . . . . . . . . . . . . . . . . . . . . . . . . . 800-428-4322
United Air Lines . . . . . . . . . . . . . . . . . . . . . . . . . . . . 800-241-6522

## AUTO RENTAL
Alamo Rent-A-Car . . . . . . . . . . . . . . . . . . . . . . . . . . .800-327-9633
Avis Rent-A-Car . . . . . . . . . . . . . . . . . . . . . . . . . . . . 800-331-1212
Budget Rent-A-Car . . . . . . . . . . . . . . . . . . . . . . . . . . 800-527-0700
Dollar Rent-A-Car . . . . . . . . . . . . . . . . . . . . . . . . . . .800-800-4000
Enterprise Rent-A-Car . . . . . . . . . . . . . . . . . . . . . . . .800-736-8222

## CREDIT CARDS
American Express . . . . . . . . . . . . . . . . . . . . . . . . . . . 800-554-AMEX
VISA . . . . . . . . . . . . . . . . . . . . . . . . . . . . . . . . . . . . . .800-336-8472
Master Card . . . . . . . . . . . . . . . . . . . . . . . . . . . . . . . .800-826-2181
Discover . . . . . . . . . . . . . . . . . . . . . . . . . . . . . . . . . . 800-347-2683

## HOTELS
Best Western . . . . . . . . . . . . . . . . . . . . . . . . . . . . . . .800-528-1234
Days Inn . . . . . . . . . . . . . . . . . . . . . . . . . . . . . . . . . . .800-325-2525
Embassy Suites . . . . . . . . . . . . . . . . . . . . . . . . . . . . . 800-362-2779
Hilton Hotels . . . . . . . . . . . . . . . . . . . . . . . . . . . . . . .800-445-8667
Marriott Hotels . . . . . . . . . . . . . . . . . . . . . . . . . . . . . 800-228-9290
Ramada Inn . . . . . . . . . . . . . . . . . . . . . . . . . . . . . . . .800-228-2828
Sheraton Inn . . . . . . . . . . . . . . . . . . . . . . . . . . . . . . . 800-325-3535
Travelodge . . . . . . . . . . . . . . . . . . . . . . . . . . . . . . . . .800-255-3050

## TRAINS
Amtrak . . . . . . . . . . . . . . . . . . . . . . . . . . . . . . . . . . . . 800-872-7245

## OTHER
American Automobile Association . . . . . . . . . . . . . . . .800-222-4357
Western Union . . . . . . . . . . . . . . . . . . . . . . . . . . . . . .800-325-6000

# NOTES